THE LIFE OF A BLACK REPUBLICAN IN TRUMP'S AMERICA

THE LIFE OF A BLACK REPUBLICAN IN TRUMP'S AMERICA

From Emancipation Proclamation to Charlottesville

DEDICATION

I dedicate this book to the late Senator John McCain: The last Republican Senator with any "Decency, Integrity, or Courage

Copyright 2019

Peter W. Sherrill

ISBN: 978-0-981-6838-7-4

Charlottesville photo shot by Stephanie Keith
Reuters photographer

Cover design by Francine Mendicino

Cover concept by Peter W. Sherrill

SPECIAL THANKS

First and foremost I would like to give a special thanks to my dear friend Dave Perozzi. Thank you for your support and for helping this vision come to fruition. You are the definition of a true friend. Glad to know you and to share such a friendship!

This next person, I have not yet had the pleasure of meeting, however, without hesitation, by the request of our mutual friend, Dave Perozzi, she immediately began to incorporate the concept for the cover of the book. I thank you from the bottom of my heart, Ms. Francine Mendicino, I see why you and Dave are lifelong friends. It has been a pleasure to have the opportunity to work with you. I thank you for creating such an awesome cover for this project!

Next, I would like to thank my editor, who is the best editor in the world, not to mention a beautiful human-being, Thank you Elsa Forsythe for all of your assistance in this project.

Last but not least by any means and without this individual, the vision for this book would have had to take on an entirely different dimension. Ms. Stephanie Keith, who actually shot the Charlottesville photo of the rally, graciously allowed us the rights to use this photograph. Thank you so much Ms. Keith. Truly appreciate your support for the completion of this project!

I also have to thank my Son for coming up with the title for this literary work! Thank you Amari Sherrill. Love you very much!

One last person, who has no idea she should be mentioned, however, her last minute walkthrough of the book made it perfect. Thank you Rachel Davis, truly appreciate you!

AUTHOR'S BIO

He never dreamed of becoming an author, although he used to kid around as he walked the "Halls of Texaco Headquarters" after the "Racial Discrimination Lawsuit" saying, "One day I am going to write a book about what really happened inside these walls!"

He definitely never thought, or would have ever believed, he would become a publisher, publishing nearly ten books in the last 10 years, mostly for other people; or sit down with Denzel Washington, preparing a foreword for an autobiography he would publish for an NBA player.

Moreover, he could have never envisioned that he would write a book about why he had left the Democratic Party to become a Republican and how 35 years after graduating with a Bachelor's of Science in Management and Economics, he would return to school to get his Master's degree in Public Administration, and begin to pursue a degree in Law at a Christian Law School, who did not seem to care about the *divine revelation* which led him to a Christian Law School or the 3.94 GPA as a Grad student, but was far more concerned with a few points on that *Standardized* test known as the *LSAT*!

Nevertheless, Peter W. Sherrill, refused to be deterred by any setbacks, even after his unsuccessful and what some may deem as insane, his attempt to run for president in 2016. His answer to those who laughed at his eccentric endeavor, is, "Look who you ended up with!"

Now Sherrill has written a new book entitled, The Life of a Black Republican in Trump's America! A book which is exponentially more explosive than his first book about the Texaco Racial Discrimination Lawsuit which, by the way, is in the Schomburg Museum Library, Harlem USA; the premiere library for Black literature and research. Sherrill cannot believe that the Party that championed the Emancipation Proclamation, is now the Party of Donald Trump and white nationalism!

Forced to face racism as a child in the sixties when forced to integrate into all white schools, along with the racism he faced in college in the South and the racism experienced at the Corporate Headquarters of Texaco Inc., nothing infuriates Sherrill more than racists and racism. Then why, some may ask, join a Party of alleged known racists?

In his last literary sequel, Exodus Why I Became A Republican, Sherrill submits that the Republican Party is not racist, at least no more than the Democrats! In his newly constructed literary work, Sherrill shares irrefutable evidence that there is one individual, specifically, who is leading the Republican Party down this path of fascism and Anti-

Semitism. Sherrill presents unprecedented and factual information in his new literary work, "The Life of A Black Republican In Trump's America," of who this individual is and where he came from. How he has gained full control of our democracy and every Branch of our government, and why he must be stopped, and why Sherrill believes he is the one who can stop him and Donald in 2020!

ABOUT THE BOOK

"The Life of A Black Republican in Trump's America" is a unique critique of the political landscape of America by an African American who joined the Republican Party in 2011, after nearly forty years as a Democrat!

The author, who allegedly claims he was instructed by God to join the Republican Party to lead the Exodus of the African American people out from the Democratic Party into the Republican Party, the Party of their ancestors, never anticipated the rise of *Jim Crow* in this alleged *Post Racial America*. The author also claims God instructed him to run for president in the 2016 election where unfortunately he was forced to watch from the side lines, as hundreds of Republicans sought the nomination.

Although extremely disappointed, even more disheartening was having to watch the Party who he believed held so much hope for the future of the African American, succumb to the racist ideology and platform of Donald Trump, who ultimately won the Republican nomination and was elected to the White House, which has proven to be a very sad day in the history of American politics.

Regardless, the author still believed then, and believes now that God has instructed him to seek the office of the presidency of the United States of America, even though there is no way on God's earth any African American would be inclined to join ranks with the Republican Party who supports a person as morally flawed and as racist as Donald Trump. As a matter of fact, watching the whole Party succumb to this racist *Jim Crow* ideology has even left the author to question his own future in the Republican Party.

Already alienated by his own people for joining the Republican Party and faced with the reality of a Party and a country that has supported, and is still supporting white nationalism by nearly every billionaire in this country, compounded by the fact that he would probably be shot and/or lynched if he were to ever attend a Trump rally, the author asks the question, how has this Party, the Party of Abraham Lincoln and the legislators of the Emancipation Proclamation, become the Party of white nationalists and Charlottesville?

What he discovers through his research of the question of how this Party of Abraham Lincoln and the Emancipation Proclamation has succumbed to white nationalists is unbelievable to say the least; that one man is responsible for the orchestration of America's decline into this racial divide. Not only is he responsible for our racial divide, he is also responsible for Brexit and the division between England and the European Union.

One man, who is referred to by the author as the *Puppet Master,* who also is the largest donor in the Republican Party, is controlling our entire Democracy, through his donations of millions to the Senate, Congress, the Supreme Court via the Federalist Society and, of course, the White House, along with his ownership of Cambridge Analytica, which is at the heart of the Russian Collusion investigation in the 2016 election. Even more disturbing is his ownership of Breitbart, the fascist, extreme right, white nationalist news medium which has allowed this extremely educated computer scientist and Ph.D, to implement his will on America's Democracy, Law and Public Policy!

It is the author's belief that the Republic, for which it stands, one nation, under God, indivisible, with liberty and justice for all, will ultimately prevail against this racist ideology, which the author submits, has no place in the Republican Party!

TABLE OF CONTENTS

CHAPTER 1

THE LIFE OF A BLACK REPUBLICAN IN TRUMP'S AMERICA

As if life wasn't hard enough already, just being a Black-man in America. Hell, since I became a Black Republican eight years ago, life has not only been hard, it has been outright crazy, and now, to make matters worse than one could ever imagine as a Black Republican, America has gone and elected Donald Trump as the 45th president. Even worse than that, as if there could even be anything worse, people are actually asking me, now that they know I am a Republican, if I actually voted for this mentally incompetent, psychotic fool! Minister or not, I have to answer emphatically, with a *"Hell f*#*#kin no!"* *Ain't no way on God's earth!* Seriously, who in the world do I look like? Do I look like that useless, pathetic *House-Negro* sitting on the Supreme

1

Court?! Really! Or, do I look like that brain dead, Brain Surgeon who is running HUD? Hell, has everyone forgotten, I sued Texaco Inc. for racial discrimination and won! Well, technically we won, however, after the feds taxed us and the lawyers got their cut and the black vultures like Jesse Jackson along with Al Sharpton, and their buddy Duval Patrick, former governor of Massachusetts, who was a nobody during that time period, capitalized off of the 35 million dollars they gave him for a manufactured, bogus, Diversity Task Force. Then, after less than one year, Texaco appointed that good *House Negro* with the title of Corporate Counsel. Twenty years later and I still can't begin to verbalize the disgust I still feel for those useless pathetic *House Negroes,* especially Duval, claiming to be the leadership for us African Americans.

Actually, the Texaco Racial Discrimination was the first stage of my disenfranchisement with Black leadership and the Democratic Party! Ultimately, shortly thereafter, working in government as Director of Emergency Services/Homeland Security, I saw such incompetency and ignorance with Black leadership and Democrats, I guess my departure after nearly forty years was imminent.

Sometimes it seriously makes me question why God gave me this crazy assignment to join the Republican Party, especially after this last presidential election in 2016. Imagine, on the one hand, Blacks want to crucify me for joining the Republican Party and now, on the other hand, these white nationalists who love and support Trump, would lynch me in a heart-beat simply because I'm Black! Now that Trump is president, there is no way on God's earth I could ever convince one Black person to ever join the Republican Party, especially after Charlottesville!

However, before this disaster, God gave me the assignment to run for POTUS in 2016 and my assignment was to lead the "Exodus" of the African American people from the Democratic plantation.

From the Party who has not done anything for us as a people for well over the last 50 years. Now, Black people will never leave that plantation after this white nationalist president has destroyed any semblance of diversity in the Republican Party and all the Republican Senators and Congressmen and women seem fine living in a "Jim Crow America." You can't even begin to imagine what it must be like, to be in my shoes, between these two factions that hate each other, compounded by trying to convince one group that they should join me and align with these extremists. One thing I do know, as sure as I know that I know, is, ain't no way I'm going back to that Democratic plantation! Yet, now, there is no way on God's earth to convince Blacks that the Republican Party is the Party for the betterment of our race. Well, I guess the first thing I will have to do is to get rid of that puppet in the White House! However, I cannot get rid of him without the support of my people. Damn, this has to be harder than God telling Jonah to go to Nineveh! To make matters

4

worse, Kanye West goes to the White House and makes a complete idiot of himself! I can hear those white nationalists, Ku Klux Klan, and Neo Nazi groups saying, *'Look at that dumb ass nigga!'* *'That's why we hate them stupid mother-fuckas!'*

Personally, I can't even begin to imagine how or why Kim Kardashian could ever marry someone that damn ignorant! However, just goes to show you what money can buy! Look at 45, do you really think Melania would have ever married Donald if he didn't have serious money? Hell no! Listen to how ignorant he sounds and look at him. Seriously, take a real good look at him! Definitely would take billions to sleep with that piece of work for the rest of your life; Til death do us part! Especially with her being a super model! However, on the flip side of that coin, ain't no super models trying to marry no Ph.D's! I wonder why? Actually, I already know, however, it is to disgusting to elaborate upon, about the exploits of men with money and power! We are actually getting

5

a front row seat to the movie playing at 1600 Pennsylvania Avenue in Washington D.C. You can have all the money in the world and it will never, ever, be able to buy you wisdom, but it sure can buy you a beautiful wife!

Nevertheless, there is a far greater problem at the forefront of our social dysfunctionality. This mission, this quest, this assignment to somehow unite these two groups, one with another. I guess one may be inclined to ask, where did I get the idea that this was my mission or purpose? For the sake of clarity and comprehension, or as Michael J. Fox would say, I guess we have to go "Back to the Future!" Actually, this entire country needs to go back to the future!

It all started when I decided to run for Mayor in my hometown of Mount Vernon, New York. I was a die-hard Democrat, "A Democrat til I die." I was working for the Mayor who appointed me to be Director of Emergency Services and Homeland

Security, approximately two years after 9/11. Previously, I was in Corporate America for the past 25 years of my life and half of those were spent at the Corporate World Headquarters of Texaco Inc., where I found myself entrenched in a racial discrimination lawsuit against the "Good Ole Boys of Texaco. After the takeover by Chevron, I left the company and shortly thereafter I ended up working in City Hall. It was a great experience, working in government, driving an official vehicle, having a gold badge, representing my hometown, the city where I was born and raised. Yet, being from corporate, I could never understand how some of the Commissioners the Mayor had appointed, who were seriously lacking intellectually, were Commissioners. I mean, they could have never worked at Texaco Inc. or in any other corporation for that fact.

Regardless of the circumstances, I just made sure I did my job well. I also could not overlook the fact that the city's schools were horrible and the city was plagued by drugs and murder. Here is the irony. For the past 20 years, the city has been run by a Black Mayor, the schools have been run by the Black Church, the City Council has been Black, the Comptroller has been Black and in spite of the fact that we have all kind of entertainers, including Denzel Washington and Felicia Rashad who are from this city and still live in this city, along with professional NBA basketball players galore, and rappers like the late great Heavy Dee and Sean P Diddy Combs, we are one of the poorest cities in one of the richest counties in America.

After the mayor lost his re-election bid and I was out as Director of Emergency Services, I began assisting the Director of Safety for the School District. I always thought one day I might be mayor, but after I saw what it was like at those press conferences, explaining double homicides, I said no thank you. Yet, after several months in the School District, and

8

seeing the horrors of the educational system, I knew it was my responsibility to say or do something. After all, my children were in private schools. I just couldn't overlook the fact that I went to public school here and graduated from high school here. Another interesting factoid is that when the Italians were running the city and the School District, things were running very smoothly. We were all getting a fairly good education, even though the Italians fought hard as all hell to resist integration.

The new mayor, who came in criticizing the previous mayor, started out his administration with having to explain 17 murders in less than 17 months. That's when I knew I had to step up to the plate. I began to think about how I could change Mount Vernon back to a city where you could walk the streets at night and wouldn't have to fear for your life, and what could I do to fix this horrible school system and create employment for this disenfranchised population? That was the plan. Things were looking good until my old boss, the former mayor, decided he was going to run again. I told my campaign manager he was going to, because I knew he loved the power that came with the position and hated that he lost the previous election, but he didn't listen and in spite of all the murders in the city during his administration, the people still loved him. I guess you could equate it to the Marion Barry syndrome. Rumor had it that all of the candidates for mayor, the incumbent, the former mayor, the Comptroller and City Council President, conspired to get me off the ballot.

Actually, that didn't really bother me as much as, none of the candidates had a plan to deal with the socio-economic woes of the city. What are you going to do about all the murders? What are you going to do about this failing school system? What are you going to do to create economic opportunities in the community for those who are basically unemployable and have no skills or trade? I had a plan, but call me selfish, I wasn't sharing it with

10

them! They wouldn't have incorporated the plans anyway, although they all wanted me to join their campaign after I didn't make the cut to be on the ballot.

Ironically, two things were going on in my life during this time period. The first was, I was now over 50 years old. The second was, now that I was over 50 years old, I needed to get my life straight with God. I'm not saying I wasn't spiritual, but, I was searching for more. I rarely went to church and after my lifelong childhood friend, whose church I used to attend, betrayed me and supported my former boss for mayor, I learned, that everyone who says they are for you, ain't!

However, I began developing a real relationship with God and was headed to the wilderness for training like Moses, and believe it or not, one day while I was praising and worshipping, God actually spoke to me. First he told me I need to leave the Democratic Party and I refused to listen! He came again to me and said, Peter, you need to switch Parties! It was crazy, but true! Finally, and the last time, He said to me, you need to switch Parties! I responded and said to myself, has God gone mad! Why would I do that? That's crazy! Plus, I'm going to win the next mayor's election! After all, I had my reputation to maintain. I'm a Democrat til I die! Right then I stopped and I asked myself the question, why? Why am I a Democrat til I die? They haven't done anything for Black people in over fifty years. The next day I went to the County and filled out the forms to become a Republican and it was one of the most exhilarating feelings I have ever experienced in my life! I understood what Herman Cain meant when he said, "He got off of that Plantation a long time ago." It's like the elephant being held by a chain and even though he can pull the chain from out of the ground, he will only go as far as the chain allows for him to go. I felt what it must have been like when my ancestors finally were free from slavery because of Abraham Lincoln and the Republican Party's

12

legislation, the Emancipation Proclamation, abolishing slavery in the United States.

Admittedly, I was a little concerned about sharing this experience with my fellow African Americans. The first real test came at a family reunion where I was going to have another book signing. This time with my book Exodus: Why I Became A Republican. I will tell you this, not one person purchased a copy of my book. All I remember them saying was, "You a Republican!?" Conversely, when I wrote my first book about the Texaco Racial Discrimination Lawsuit, everyone wanted a copy! I don't think I even had enough to sell to everyone!

Truth of the matter is, was and still is the fact, that as my relationship with God was continuing to grow, there was no way on God's earth I could remain a Democrat. Their values just didn't line up with my values as a *child* of the Most High God! All I know is that becoming a Republican was like eating "manna: from heaven, at least before this debacle that has taken place with Donald Trump in 2016. It's insane! I never thought for one minute that when I joined the Republican Party in 2011, I would be so ashamed about the direction of this Party!

Now, it will take a miracle for Blacks to even consider leaving the Democratic Party. How on God's earth did this Party, the Party that crafted the Emancipation Proclamation, become the Party of the white nationalists in Charlottesville? Truth be told, white nationalists are the descendants of those racist Democrats in the South! They are the same ones who killed Abraham Lincoln! And with his assassination, the biggest mistake in the history of the United States transpired! Andrew Johnson, A damn southern Democrat, Lincoln's Vice President, yes, Lincoln chose a damn Southern Democrat for his Vice President, who, after Lincoln's assassination, became President and began to repeal and replace everything the Reformation that was taking place in this country had achieved! First and foremost,

14

starting with the "Black Codes." Ironically, I had never, ever heard of the Black Codes, until I was in Grad school doing research on a paper. I could not believe my eyes when I saw what the Black codes represented! All I could say to myself was, those damn Democrats! Actually, for the record, it was the Republicans who tried to impeach Johnson, but lost by one vote. The more I read and learned about the Democrats I began thinking to myself, I have to be a freaking idiot to be a Democrat! I mean, the horrors go on and on and on! "Google it!"

CHAPTER 2

FROM EMANCIPATION PROCLAMATION TO CHARLOTTESVILLE

The history of the Republican Party is an interesting one for African Americans because we were first Republicans before we were hoodwinked and bamboozled into becoming Democrats. Even Dr. Martin Luther King, Jr.'s father was a Republican. The question now is, if we were Republicans before we became Democrats, surely the White nationalists were not in the Republican Party. It is even more obvious that they were not in the Republican Party before, during or after the Civil War. First of all, they are proponents of the Confederate flag. They were vehemently against the abolition of slavery. Therefore they were against Lincoln and the

Emancipation Proclamation, which manifested from the Republican Party. Their ancestors also fought and died attempting to preserve slavery and probably would turn over in their graves if they knew their descendants were now Republicans.

Another irony is their alliance with Neo Nazis. Again, didn't their forefathers fight against Hitler and defeat the Third Reich? And now they are marching side by side making a mockery of American Democracy, while ready to claim allegiance to the American flag, carrying Confederate and Neo Nazi flags in America. Somehow, I classify that as a little more anti-American, in comparison to taking a knee during the singing of the National Anthem. However, I absolutely do not support Kaepernick either. They both dishonor the American flag and American Democracy! If anything, you would think that Blacks and Whites would be united because of the fact that the one million Blacks who fought in WWII made all the difference in the defeat of Hitler and the Third Reich. For all who may disagree, just ask General Patton. Yet, when we came home in victory, a German soldier could sit down at a lunch counter in the South and order a burger where an American Black soldier would not be served because of the Jim Crow laws. Can you even imagine what it must have been like for a Black soldier to try and get access to a G.I. Bill from a bank in the South? For those who don't know, it was a Black man who invented the gas mask used in WWI, and because of this invention thousands of lives were saved on the battlefields during this war. Blacks and Whites have both fought and died on the battlefields defending America, the land of the free and the home of the brave, yet you continue to let racial hatred dictate your actions and emotions. We need to find the same camaraderie we shared on the battlefields fighting for truth, justice and the American way, when we come back home in victory. Honestly, in spite of the fact that we had to live through the brutality of being slaves in this

18

country, you will find we believe in many of the same truths of the Constitution of the United States; especially, "We hold these truths to be self -evident, that all men are created equal." Our unification is essential to America reaching the next level of its greatness. We were the ones who fought side by side in great numbers and with great pride for the American flag and the Democracy it represents. No other group or nationality has shed the amount of blood that Blacks and Whites have shed in order to maintain this freedom. These other groups were not there on the battlefields of Germany. They were not there on the battlefields against Japan. They do not know the price that has been paid by our ancestors who registered by the millions to fight for this freedom that even the Neo Nazis experience in America. Tell me, in what other country can you come, wave a flag from another nation in direct opposition to the country you live in and your family has died for, fighting against their quest for world dominance and the destruction of America's freedom and democracy, and our constitution protects their rights? Tell me where? Name one country! Only in America! And yet, we have this freedom and democracy because we defeated the Neo Nazis' attempt to rule the world. Yet, now, Nazis come here and seek to align with you because of a past mentality of racial hatred, which for all intents and purposes, if it had continued, they assuredly would have been victorious in WWI and definitely in WWII. However, our ancestors fought and destroyed neo-nazism! Do you think for one minute the Confederate flag would be allowed in a victorious Germany? They are actually playing on your weakness and ignorance as a people. They can't even hold a protest like that in Germany, so why are you bringing this nonsense to America? However, America is the only country where you can hold a protest even if it's in direct contrast to America. Can't go to Russia with that nonsense. Putin ain't having it! Therefore, if they don't have you to join them, who do they have? Take that same asinine mentality back to where it came from, Europe! Isn't this the reason why your forefathers left British rule in the first place! Isn't this why they crafted the Constitution and the Declaration of Independence? Why do you want to align with those who are in direct opposition to everything your forefathers fought for? Because you share a common denominator of racial hatred? That's the only variable connecting the two factions, except maybe their blood that was shed by your ancestors of their ancestors on the battlefields of the World Wars. Thank God for this victory! God Bless America now and always. It would appear, anyone against the United States of America is actually against God. However, as long as we continue to support these subversive organizations, who remain steadfast in their hatred of America, the potential for America's democracy will never reach the splendor of the vision that the forefathers crafted in those awe-inspiring documents! Following WWII, America stood as the greatest nation in the entire world. There was not anything America could not achieve. Yet, while standing as the greatest nation in the world, the world also saw America as the greatest hypocrite because of its racial hatred towards Blacks. No other ethnicity has been so persecuted, and we have worked for free for this country, we have fought side by side with you for this country, even without guns while in combat, but because of this continued racial hatred, you are willing to jeopardize everything this nation stands for. What's even worse is you claim to represent Christ, and since the Emancipation Proclamation which by the way, was crafted by the Republican Party, you have left your Party of origin, (Democratic Party), to now bring that cancerous mentality over to the Republican Party. Since the majority of you were in the South, and still supporting the Confederacy, that definitely puts you at extreme odds with the Republican Party.

Apparently, as the migration of African Americans over to the Democrats began to seriously take root with the election of the first Black mayor in a major city as a Democrat in the 1960's - Cleveland, Ohio, to be exact - a mass exodus by whites from the Democratic Party to the Republican Party began to take place in America. However, during this mass exodus they also brought that Jim Crow mentality. Initially, it was not so obvious, because the symptoms were like stage one cancer. Today, it has become extremely blatant as more and more of these carriers of this cancerous mentality began to infiltrate the Party of Lincoln. And now, the Republican Party has become as deadly as stage four cancer and is facing imminent death unless it gets extensive radiation and chemotherapy to eradicate this right wing cancerous tumor of white nationalism! Today, in the 21st century, who would have ever believed that the Party which was once the Party of Lincoln, is now the party of the Grand Wizard and the Ku Klux Klan! Who would ever believe the Evangelical Right is responsible for fueling such a divisive, Anti-Christian, satanic movement! I remember the first time I was invited to attend one of the Westchester

County Tea Party's meeting in White Plains, New York. One of the members took great exception to the chapter in my book, (EXODUS: Why I Became A Republican), about the Tea Party. She vehemently protested and said "We are not like that!" She also challenged me to come to one of their meetings, which I eventually did. I remember walking into this dimly lit room in the back of a pub. In my mind I was saying, Peter, what have you gotten yourself into? She then introduced me to the president and said, "He wrote a book and you should see the things he said about the Tea Party!" All eyes were on me. I was thinking, I wonder if this is how Blacks felt going to their *Pic-Nics*, which was code for pick-a-nigga to lynch for their gathering. Probably why the Senate candidate from Mississippi felt so comfortable saying she would have a front row seat to a lynching. It makes me question how on God's earth you can proclaim to be a Christian and then so casually murder? Sounds more like something Satan would do! Well, the president just simply said, "You should come again and share your book with the group." I said, "Seriously!" I was caught off guard a little, because I wasn't sure if he was really serious. In my mind I was saying, this is the last time I would ever be coming to a Tea Party meeting. A couple of weeks later, wouldn't you know, the president asked me to come and speak about my book at the next meeting. I contacted the woman who invited me to the first meeting to see if she would be attending and she told me no! Damn, I said, how am I going to get out of this debacle? There is no way I'm going there without having someone with me. I figured I should at least let someone know what I was doing and where I was going and so I did. At the time I was doing my internship for my Masters at the Boys & Girls Club in Mount Vernon. I told my friend who was the Executive Director, that I was going to White Plains to discuss my book with the Tea Party. He said with disbelief, "The Tea Party!?" I said "Yup!" He looked at me and said "Yeah, Okay!" As if it would be his last time seeing me. Honestly, I had no idea about what exactly I would say to these people! When I arrived, the president and I greeted each other and he told me the order in which the evening would proceed. First and foremost, they do the Pledge of Allegiance. Actually, I thought that was pretty cool. Shortly after, their guests who were running for office got up to address the group, asking for their support for their campaign. It was one of the most fascinating experiences of my life. The questions they asked were sharp, insightful, and specific to upcoming legislation. I was in awe! When politicians come to speak in our communities, they never answer questions that are serious like that, I guess, because we don't even know about questions that are so specific to legislation that are going to affect our life and economic future. All they usually give us is "keep hope alive" as a slogan. Big difference! All I knew was that I was developing an entirely new perspective and respect for this group known as the Westchester County Tea Party! Now the moment has come. I am being introduced to the group. I take a deep breath and go up to the podium and reflect on something my professor told us about public speaking. I look at my audience and said something hilarious! At least I thought it was, but was not exactly sure how they would respond. I said good evening and I thanked the president for allowing to share my book with the group. Then I said it. It was really a racist statement, but it was true. So I said to them, "You know what? When I first received the invitation to come and speak to the group about my book, I thought I was coming to a meeting to see the Grand Wizard!" Believe it or not, they burst out laughing and so did I! It was funny as hell! We laughed for a good minute! Then I said, "However, after listening to the questions you guys were asking the gentlemen who are seeking your support for their campaigns, I have a tremendous amount of respect for you! The politicians who come and talk to the people in my community wouldn't stand a chance in hell if they came to talk to you guys. You ask tough questions about specific issues and legislation that impact your communities. I hope that one day I can get my people to ask questions like that and know about the legislation that is being voted on that affects the community.

Needless to say that when I finished speaking, I got a standing ovation. However, something greater happened. An older White woman came over to me and began to ask me a couple of questions. She asked if I knew Roy Innis and did he have any influence on my decision to become a Republican? I said, "I have heard of him, but not at all." Then she asked me about Herman Cain. Again, I said, "I know who he is, but, no way." Then she said something that made becoming a Republican worth its weight in gold. She said, "It's good you listened to God!" At that precise moment, it all made sense. Here I was talking to people I perceived as racists, yet were anything but. They believed in God for the most part and believed in America and our Democracy. I became really good friends with the president and some other members and they admired my courage to become a Republican living in a community that was mostly Black. All I did was do as God had instructed and my life was taking on a whole new meaning. The next day when I spoke to the Executive Director of the Boys & Girls Club in Mount Vernon, he asked "How did it go?" I said, "It was amazing!" Just goes to show the dangers of stereotyping people.

Now I am officially a member of the Westchester County Tea Party, going to different group meetings and sharing why I became Republican. The fascinating part is that when I share that God instructed me to do this, they really get it. They truly understand. They also feel as though it is awesome. Conversely, when I try to tell Black people that God instructed me to do this, they look at me like I have lost my mind! That is probably because Blacks do not realize how indoctrinated we have become by the Democrats and the Black leadership. It's for that same reason why everybody knows that we will only vote for Democrats. Although I will say Republicans have not made it easy because of the racist perception they tend to generate, especially now that the Party has been fully blown with stage four cancer from this tumor of white nationalism. The one fault of the Republican Party is the fact they are just like the symbol that represents the Party, the elephant. All it takes is for one elephant to decide to go in another direction and the rest just follow. What is even more interesting is that this white nationalist agenda has been spearheaded by just one man!

Throughout history, it has always been one man. It was that one man that led Germany down the path of white nationalism. The descendants of those who have fought and died for this nation are now going down that same path and aligning themselves with this ideology and it is destroying this nation as we speak! One man has orchestrated this fiasco and Donald is just his pawn! They always look for a pawn, a puppet, someone who is more or less an idiot! Actually, couldn't have asked for a better candidate to push forward such an agenda. This is why I was so surprised at the reception I received from the Tea Party. I now realize that the perception of the Republican Party does not fit all Republicans. For example, I remember inviting the guys to a book signing I was having for an author whose autobiography I had published. Not only did they attend, there were more members from the Tea Party than from the community. Actually, the book signing was for the Executive Director of the Boys & Girls Club and, boy oh boy, was he shocked to see all these members from the Tea Party. Even he had to re-evaluate his perception about the Tea Party. Shortly thereafter, a few of the guys came to me and said they would like to start an entrepreneurial program at the Mount Vernon Boys & Girls Club. Now, the Chief Professional Officer of the Club had to think twice about the Tea Party. The members of the Tea Party also bought a table for the Mount Vernon Boys & Girls Club's annual gala. Don't sound like white nationalists to me. Even I was also compelled to re-evaluate. Then I realized why God gave me this insane assignment to become a Republican. It was to build a bridge between the two groups and weed out those stereotypes from both sides of the aisle.

Honestly, I was starting to have a ball sharing with people in my community, that I was no longer a Democrat! They would look at me in disbelief. I would say, "Nope, I can't sign your petition." I remember the mayor, who was my former boss, had me on his radio show to discuss my new book EXODUS: Why I Became A Republican and all he could say was, "A Republican!" However, as far as I was concerned, I no longer had to vote for politicians who were incompetent and had no intention whatsoever of improving the conditions for the people in my hometown, Mount Vernon, New York. I know they would never be able to stand in front of the members of the Westchester County Tea Party and sell the garbage they were selling to the

Blacks in my community. I would love to hear them try to explain to the Tea Party, if this was their community, how in a city that is 75% African American and 99% Democrat, why there aren't people from the community working on all these *multi-million dollar* construction projects going on in the community? Why aren't there any individuals from our community working on the Bridge for Andrew Cuomo's father? However, come election time, all these politicians from the Democratic Party run down to Mount Vernon because of their loyalty to blindly vote for Democrats only. Hate to say it, but the members of the Tea Party would run them out of town! Hate to say this also: maybe we could learn some things from these people in the Tea Party! I know I sure did.

I'll never forget the evening after one of the meetings with the Westchester County Tea Party, and as we were wrapping up, a conversation started up about Lyndon Johnson. So I curiously inquired, what about

LBJ? They look at me in astonishment, like, you're Black and you don't know about LBJ? Here I am boasting about being in Grad School, studying Public Administration and I don't know anything about LBJ except the Great Society. Then the president of the group said, LBJ voted against every Civil Rights Bill that ever came across his desk when he was Senator in Texas! I was in total disbelief and he could see that I didn't believe what he just said, so he told me to look it up. And so I did! And it was true! You have to understand what was happening to me. I was discovering truth. It was beginning to make more and more sense as to why God keep pushing me to switch Parties. It was like God was saying, so what, I know who they are, but there are some things you are going to need to know and only they can teach you. Then after that discovery, I found out that Woodrow Wilson, our 28th president, refused to sign an anti-lynching bill. Another damn Democrat! The more I learned, the more I began to realize that not only was I supposed to learn from my new friends in the Tea

34

Party, but I was also to take this information and share it with my people, so they could stop and think about who and why they are voting for these Democrats, over and over, again and again, who have hardly done anything to improve their community.

Imagine what it was like when I would tell people that Goldman Sachs was the second largest contributor to Barack's campaign. We were so in love with having the first ever Black President that we didn't pay attention to all the warning signs and that is why we are worse off today than we ever were. However, other groups are flourishing! Not to say that Barack isn't ten times better than Trump, yet, the same blindness with which we followed Barack, is the same blindness they follow Trump. They don't give a damn what Trump does or doesn't do. They will follow him off the edge of a cliff! We did the same thing when it came to Barack. However, remember, Goldman Sachs was the second largest contributor to Barack's first campaign. It was by design and once they knew he was in agreement with the $750 billion bailout, recommended by Bush's Treasury Secretary, who also happened to be the former President and CEO of, that's right, Goldman Sachs, then the campaign money came and Hilary was defeated. However, with Donald, it's a lot darker. As I previously stated, one man orchestrated this whole Trump fiasco. One man, trying to control all the world's economies! One man, promoting hate and division and white nationalism! One man who knew that this would incite all the deep inner prejudices that lay dormant inside white people, waiting to be awakened. Just like they used Barack to manipulate us, they are using Trump to manipulate whites also. They study all of our behaviors and they know all of the areas, through extensive research, that will trigger us to revolt and protest! This time, all they wanted to do is to get that trillion dollar tax cut through and who better than Donald to do their bidding. It is very interesting how they get us to vote for things that will never benefit us. Malcolm X used to say to the Blacks in the community about the Democrats, "You've been hoodwinked and bamboozled." Well, guess what white America, you've been played like fools because of one man's quest for control. The answer to the mystery is, find out who Steve Bannon's boss is. I say this to say, don't feel bad, they did the same thing to us Blacks! You should have seen how many T-shirts with the image of Martin Luther King Jr. and Barack Obama were being purchased in Harlem and throughout the country. Look at how many MAGA hats they sold. It's all propaganda! You fell for it and so did we. Now we need to figure out how to stop them! I am hoping that the unification and friendship I found with my constituents in the Tea Party will transfer to a major unification between the two groups. The day that takes place will be the day that America will truly reach the highest pinnacles of success. Also know that there will be those from both Parties who will fight like hell to prevent this from happening, because they will soon be unemployed, and honestly,

I believe it will be the end of the Democrats. Once Blacks awaken to the fact that they have been played like fools by the Democrats for the last fifty years, they will come to find, as I have found, that the Republican Party which was the Party of our ancestors, is the Party that is more likely to benefit us in the future, once we overcome these racists who have infiltrated the Republican Party. There is a good reason why Blacks such as, Ida B. Wells, Booker T. Washington, Martin Luther King, Sr. were Republicans, mainly because of the racist disposition of the Southern Democrats. Even while Barack was beginning to win popularity over Hillary, Bill Clinton's racist upbringing from Arkansas came to the surface. John F. Kennedy did not particularly care for Martin Luther King, Jr. Neither did Lyndon Johnson! This is why an exodus from the Democratic Party needs to take place in America, but with Donald being the puppet of the one man who really controls the right wing, I'm not sure how this will eventually play out. They know that as long as you feed these people *Jim Crow*, they will always come to dine. Therefore, it behooves this one man, to ensure his power, that he keeps feeding the Republican right, *Jim Crow*. I guess it is time to take a look at this one man who is Trump's Puppet Master! The interesting thing about the "Puppet Master is that he isn't any different from all previous tyrants throughout history. He is no different from Osama Bin Laden. He is no different from Adolph. He is no different from the Ayatollah, Kim in North Korea, Putin, or Assad in Syria. All extremists! I remember when Malcolm X went to his first pilgrimage to Mecca. Since he had joined the Nation of Islam, all he was ever taught was that the white man was the devil. It was easy for him to accept that, especially because of the white men who killed his father. However, during his pilgrimage something happened that changed his entire perspective. He saw white, blond-haired, blue eyed Muslims. Yet, it was one man who led him to believe this ideology. No different from this one man leading whites down this path of white nationalism.

CHAPTER 3

Robert Leroy Mercer

The Puppet Master

WHO? Who the hell is Robert Leroy Mercer? I bet you the majority of the people walking around with MAGA hats on have no idea of who this individual is. To start, he is the owner of your right-wing media outlet, Breitbart. I bet you some of the people walking around with MAGA hats on, have never heard of Breitbart. However, the real danger is with the people who follow this propaganda. All you need is one elephant in the community to start the conversation and the rest will follow. It's not that the information isn't true, however, the polarization of a race of people always poses a danger to America's Democracy. That's what allowed Hitler to polarize

41

Germans against the Jews! And who had to fight to eliminate that threat? America! Yet, in 2018/2019, here we are again fighting against the same cancerous, destructive ideology right here on our soil, because there is a group of people who believe they are superior to all other races. If any group of people who should feel superior to any other race, it should be the Africans who ruled during the time of the Roman Empire, who built the Pyramids that still have not been decoded. However, if you are feeling left out and your concept of the American Dream is being attained by foreigners and even worse, illegal immigrants, then yes, it is easy to sell a message of hate and we need to take back our country. That is what Breitbart has done! What Breitbart doesn't tell you is that during George W. Bush's administration, America exported/outsourced over four million jobs and you geniuses voted for George twice. Well, really once. We all know he stole the first election with the help of his brother Jeb, then the Governor of Florida! Can you imagine! America was about to elect that scum to the presidency! The only reason why he wasn't elected was because the "Puppet Master" did not want him there. He knew he couldn't do his bidding, especially pertaining to immigration, because he was married to a Hispanic. However, if he wanted Jeb to be president, he would have been!

Actually, we probably have Trump to thank for knocking Jeb out of the race. I remember during one debate, Trump looked down at Jeb and said, "The last thing this country needs is another Bush!" Personally, I could not have agreed more. Jeb was going around raising enormous sums of money, and when he finally announced, he had far more money than all the other contenders. And because he had more money than everyone else, he believed, just as all the other 100 Republican candidates, that he would win by default, because they all also believed, that whoever had the most money would ultimately win the Republican Primary. As for myself, I was hoping and praying that someone with a Super Pac would see my website Securing America 2016, and bio, and would empathize with my new found revelation, realization and transformation from the Democratic Party. After nearly 40 years as a Democrat, I longed to share my profound political and spiritual awakening which had led me to the most profound enlightenment ever, in my entire life, that becoming a Republican was the key to political freedom for African Americans. I also figured, with my extensive background and training in Homeland Security, along with my educational background in Public Administration and 25 years experience in Corporate America, I would make a great Presidential candidate for the Republican Party.

One Super PAC, that's all I would have needed to successfully launch this campaign. Wouldn't it have been ironic if Robert Mercer would have supported my vision for the country and backed my campaign instead of sending this country into peril under Trump? Imagine, a white nationalist supporting an

African American as a Presidential candidate for the United States of America, for the Republican Party! However, truth of the matter is, there really isn't a place in the Republican Party, or America for that matter, for such a poisonous, cancerous mentality. So in retrospect, I guess I would have had to refuse any support from the *Puppet Master,* even if it meant I could have been well on my way to becoming the next POTUS. Obviously, Trump didn't refuse Mercer's super PAC and has been dominated by the *Puppet Master,* along with all the numerous other Republican candidates he controls with his contributions to their campaigns.

One thing I do know for sure, which is the whole point, pertaining to the *Puppet Master.* He is very powerful and extremely influential. He is not as visible as the Koch brothers, however, he is more powerful than the Koch brothers, and not just because of his right-wing news media Breitbart. His rise to power far exceeds the reach of Breitbart.

Make no mistake, Robert Leroy Mercer is an extremely intelligent individual. Why else would he back an egomaniac!? He needed someone who was not that intelligent and could appeal to the segment of the population that was either ignorant or uneducated. And just for the record, Robert L. Mercer is a computer scientist and a developer in early artificial intelligence. He is also the CEO of the elite and exclusive hedge fund, Renaissance Technologies and also has a Ph.D from the University of Illinois at Urbana-Champaign. That's just the tip of the iceberg!

He has become one of the largest donors to campaigns for the Republican Party. He fueled the Trump campaign with his money and got rid of Paul Manafort, imported his main man and white nationalists supreme promoter, Steve Bannon, along with Kellyanne Conway, to run the Trump campaign. So, for all of you Trump supporters who think you are supporting Donald, all you are really doing is supporting a puppet. Robert Leroy Mercer, is actually running this country! Actually, he is impacting the whole global economy. You must understand, Mercer is a computer scientist who ran programs for the Air Force, used to work for IBM and started a hedge fund called Renaissance. Renaissance runs computer algorithms to determine what and when to buy and/or sell. So, in essence, while you are on *E-trade, trying to buy or sell, Mercer will have run thousands of computerized algorithms per second before you can even sell one share. What's even more interesting is that the only way you can trade or do business with Renaissance is you have to be an employee or have special relationship with Mercer. I wonder how many of you who are reading his right wing nationalists newspaper, Breitbart, run by Steve Bannon, (Harvard MBA graduate) actually have access to Renaissance? Probably none of you! Yet, you are all walking around wearing MAGA hats, and Mercer doesn't give a damn about you. You are just promoting his agenda.

However, before he used you, he practiced on England first. Have you ever heard of Brexit? The reason why I ask, is because I'm not sure what the intelligence level is for some of you people, because you really have to be unaware in order to be used like this. However, I will say this: don't feel too bad, they got us really good also, with Barack Obama! They exploit our deepest emotional sentiments, and then bombard us with messaging. "Make America Great Again!" Obama's was "Change has come to America!" Really! What change? Ain't a damn thing has changed in America, if you are Black! I guarantee you, if you were to ask any average Black American, who was the second largest contributor to Barack Obama's campaign in 2008, they would not have a clue! When I tell them it was Goldman Sachs, and that George Bush's Treasury Secretary was recently the President and CEO of Goldman Sachs before he became Treasury Secretary, Blacks are left dumbfounded. They cannot believe how they have been "hoodwinked and bamboozled," as Malcolm X used to say. So again I ask, how long are we going to allow this elite group to continue to politically manipulate us?

England is in such a quagmire now because of the Brexit referendum held on leaving the European Union. Neither side knows what in the world to do, and the entire global economy, except China, are hopelessly waiting to determine what they should do next! I know it's unbelievable that one man could wreak such havoc and chaos, yet, Mercer orchestrated this whole ordeal through his algorithms and data mining! Remember, Mercer developed programs for early artificial intelligence. He's like the mad computer scientist, like in Pinky and the Brain! Diabolical! Yet, Brexit was just the beginning. Remember the fiasco that surfaced about Facebook and Cambridge Analytica? Well, guess who owns Cambridge Analytica? Robert Leroy Mercer. Guess who is Cambridge Analytica's Vice President? Steve Bannon. What's even more interesting is Mark Zuckerberg's denial to the Senate about knowing anything about the targeted ads that ran on Facebook targeting people they believed would support Trump: and he is the President and CEO of Facebook! Isn't it just a tad bit ironic that people from Cambridge Analytica sit on Facebook's Board! England has actually called Zuckerberg back to testify before Parliament because they have discovered that he lied to the British Parliament! However, no one is even mentioning the *Puppet Master!* It is simply amazing to me how Robert Leroy Mercer continues to go unnoticed! Sounds like something straight out of the movie, Mission Impossible: Ghost Protocol. However, you must also remember, Mercer does have a Ph.D! He really is that intelligent! I don't know about you guys, but I'm tired of being their pawns in this game of chess! It's obvious, they need for us to hate each other! Just in case you may have forgotten, it was American Blacks and Whites on the battlefields of Germany that led to the defeat of Hitler and America's rise as the number one military and economic power of the world. However, racism still prevailed over the victory of war due to *Jim Crow's* refusal to die, especially in the South! This toxic cancer which remains entrenched in the hearts and souls of those racists in the South who were once die hard members of the Democratic Party, have attached themselves and this cancerous ideology to the Republican Party, the Party of Lincoln. It will do anything to survive. It is what gives Breitbart relevance! And now these cancerous cells have mutated into the brainchild of Robert Leroy Mercer. Mercer's reach does not stop there either. Have you ever heard of the Federalist Society? Who are the Federalist Society, you may ask? The Federalist Society is a Think-Tank based in the Nation's Capitol, comprised of conservatives and libertarians seeking to control all aspects of the law of the land under the premise that the law should be

51

in accordance or based upon the original interpretation of the United States Constitution. It is also one of the nation's most influential legal organizations, more than likely based upon the funding provided by none other than Robert Leroy Mercer, "The Puppet Master!" The Federalist Society is where the mentoring of young conservative lawyers who aspire to rise to power through government jobs, political appointments, elected political officials for Senate and Congress, and federal judgeships under Republican presidents, are groomed and selected. All who are now under the full control and influence of none other than Robert Leroy Mercer, who is presently, the largest donor to the Republican Party. What this actually means is that Robert Mercer controls all the major elected officials in the Party of the Legislative branch of government, the Executive branch which is under Trump, who he, not Vladimir totally controls - contrary to what so many people believe, and with his sphere of financial influence of the Federalist

Society, he now also controls the Judiciary branch of our government and democracy! The Federalist Society is the group who selects and recommends those individuals for the Supreme Court! Mercer is definitely in control of those recommendations! I told you from the outset that this man was extremely intelligent. Just in case you forgot, Mercer has a Ph.D and he is, or was a computer scientist who dealt with the early phases of artificial intelligence. He wrote computer programs for the Air Force and has a hedge fund which has catapulted him into billionaire status! The main difference between Mercer and all these other wealthy donors, besides the fact that he is 100 times smarter than all of them combined, is the fact Mercer made his money, whereas the Koch Brothers probably acquired their wealth from 'old money.'

However, herein lies the problem, or as we say in Public Administration, the dichotomy! As amazing as it may sound, that one man has all this power, influence and control of the United States government because of his extreme right-wing views through his news medium Breitbart, which is no different in extremism than ISIS, Hitler, Stalin, Napoleon or Mussolini, Robert Leroy Mercer, is a threat to the Republic and a threat to our Democracy! His extreme right views which are not only fascist, they are ungodly! Remember, communist societies were and still are godless, and the main ingredient that we hold dear, or used to hold dear as to why we were better than those godless societies and made us better than those societies, was because we believed in God and believed in God Bless America! Isn't it so very ironic that we pledge allegiance to the flag of the United States of America, then defend fascism, the very ideology our forefathers fought against and defeated. Yet Robert Leroy Mercer is resurrecting this toxic, cancerous, divisive ideology in America, and the Republican Party, the Party which set America on its path to become the greatest Empire ever, because of its belief in God! With his money he has infiltrated the Republican Party with this toxic ideology and is destroying the only Party which is capable of keeping America superior to all other nations. Now he is resuming his quest throughout Europe, through his other puppet, Steve Bannon! There is no room for Mercer in the Republican Party. However, I fear it may be too late, because they all have drank and have become drunk with the wine of his billions of dollars he has used to gain control of all facets of our democracy.

While we are focused on fascism and racism in America, Mercer has just recently purchased thousands of shares from the Vanguard Growth Fund ETF. The fund is a diversification index of the largest growth stocks of United States Companies and represents the largest capitalization companies in the United States equity market. You may think this is just thousands of shares of stock from Vanguard, but in actuality, it is shares from thousands of growth funds, which "The Puppet Master" has just bought. Big difference. My question to all of those fighting for the resurrection of fascism is, did Mercer include you in on this deal? Doubt it! As I have previously stated, they need us to continually focus upon hating each other. While we are fighting over racism in America and an alleged post racial America, which was nothing than more propaganda, Mercer and his elite group of investors in the hedge fund he created for his own purpose, Renaissance Hedge Fund; He is making billions and billions of dollars at our expense and ignorance. Once again I ask, how long will we continue to be their pawns? Oh, by the way, did you hear about the insider trading deal Mercer just pulled off under Renaissance Hedge Fund, using the American Federation of Teachers' pension? Renaissance has been guilty of partnering with corporations who are making money off the Trump administration's policies at the southern border and I am sure this is why Trump is fighting so hard for the Border Wall. First of all, Mexico damn sure *ain't* paying for "The Wall!" Just for the record, who do you think is going to have to pay the five billion for this wall? The American taxpayer. And remember, this is just the initial phase. In other words, while they are profiting from the detention centers being built at the border where they are holding illegal immigrants, they will also be profiting from the wall.

Now, if I was investing in detention centers at the southern border and making billions of dollars from this new policy, do you think I would actually want it to stop? Doubt it! Now that the American Federation of Teachers have found out that Renaissance and other Hedge Funds have been using their pensions to fund these detention centers, all hell is about to break loose! My question is, do you think Mercer had some insight into the policy on detention centers from the White House, or has Mercer influenced the policies coming out of the White House? Either way, if you don't think so, then you are more naive than I thought!

Nevertheless, detention centers at the southern border, or the wall, doesn't even begin to compare to the trillion dollar tax cut those puppets in the Senate have just given to Mercer and his billionaire cronies. Again I ask, who do you people believe has to pay for this tax cut? Once again, while we are arguing over immigration, Obamacare, and other social matters that keep us distracted from what is really going on, "The Puppet Master" sends his puppets, Steve Bannon and Donald Trump to keep the world distracted. We were duped into believing the Senate had to have this trillion dollar tax cut get passed to validate Trump's presidency! And who do you think that trillion dollars was for? For you? For me? No my friends, it was for the one percent, who have hoodwinked and bamboozled us once again into giving them hundreds of billions of dollars and we can't even get a loan from the bank or increase in our pay! On top of that, corporations are beginning to lay off workers again, not to mention we have thousands of homeless Vets committing suicide every single day at alarming rates! What's even more interesting is, if you try to increase any funding for education, the far right goes out of their mind! Now that's sick! Or just damn ignorant! As I have previously stated, they need us to continually focus upon hating each other. While we are fighting over racism in America and an alleged post racial America, which is nothing but more propaganda, Mercer and his elite group of investors in Renaissance Hedge Fund continue to make billions and billions of dollars.

However, when you've been brainwashed, you will believe that only Blacks and Latinos are on welfare, when in reality, there are more white people on welfare than both of those groups combined. Then, they have you believe that in order to make America strong, they need a trillion dollar tax cut! Do you realize what a trillion dollars is? It is my hope, when I finish showing and explaining how they are using our hostility towards each other and against one another, you will begin to take a closer look at this highway robbery that is taking place on each and every American who has to pay the taxes for these financial exploits in Washington and Wall Street! Black, White or Latino, we all have to pay, if you are a legal resident of the United States!

CHAPTER 4

THE TRILLION DOLLAR TAX CUT

What is a trillion dollars? A trillion dollars is 999 billion, 999 million, 999 thousand, 999 dollars and 99 cents. The reason for sharing this number in this format is because it is my goal and objective to help you see clearly what is being done by these wealthy group of individuals while we pay for their exploits. First it was their toxic assets in 2008. Now it is the **"Trillion Dollar Tax Cut."**

Let's look at an example. Let us pretend you were to receive $100,000 (one hundred thousand dollars) a year, without having to pay taxes or any other expenses. In ten years you would have earned one million dollars. In one hundred years, you would have earned one hundred million dollars. Follow very closely now. It would take you one thousand years at $100,000 per year, to earn just one billion dollars. That's right! It would take one thousand years to make one billion dollars! The irony is, you will never be able to earn $100,000 per year without any other expenses, so it would probably take the average American Taxpayer 10,000 years to make one billion dollars, because the average American Taxpayer only earns approximately $60,000 per year before taxes!

Can you even imagine! So, what on God's earth could anybody possibly need with $999 billion dollars, when it would take at least, one thousand years to make one billion dollars?

Yet, we have just authorized this Senate to give the one per cent this astronomical sum of funding, and for what? Because they need it? Or maybe it's because they want to give it to the American taxpayer! Or is it simply because we are so busy fighting with each other, and ignorant enough to give it to them?

It's because we are ignorant enough to give it to them, again! We already gave them $750 billion dollars in 2008 because of the alleged toxic assets in the mortgage industry they all invested in knowingly. Ask billionaire Warren Buffet! He knew! He let them use his Moody's Bond rating system, (which he owns) to give those toxic assets a Triple A rating, even though they knew there wasn't any financial backing for it. And because of the insurance regulations, legally they would not be able to sell this junk to all their global investors. However, since Moody can give a Triple A rating, without having to report to regulators, they were able to sell this junk to the whole entire world and the world bought it because Moody gave it a Triple A rating. Compounded also by the fact, that Americans were losing their jobs because of the massive outsourcing in Corporate America, during George's administration. What they also didn't tell us, the American people who would have to pay for this criminal fiasco, was that they took an additional 1.2 trillion dollars to give to the banks on top of the $750 billion.

While you are trying to comprehend these numbers, just keep in mind that it will take at least, one thousand years to earn just one billion dollars. So while we argue over the extreme white nationalist ideology, gay rights, Obamacare, climate change, equal rights and civil rights, these bastards are robbing the American Taxpayer blind! Remember, the American Taxpayer is any American citizen, Black, White, Latino, Democrat, Republican, Independent, etc... They are screwing us all, and if we don't get past these issues which keep us divided, they will continue screwing us until we are dead and buried!

Personally, this is why I was trying so vehemently to be heard in 2016; that, and also for the grave concern for the security of our nation. Hey, the truth of the matter is that I was an Economics major in college and spent 25 years in Corporate America. And after leaving Corporate America I became Director of Emergency Services and trained extensively with First Responders from all across this Nation, at specialized facilities throughout this Country and with NYPD, for the War on Terror. Yup, I'm like a Black James Bond!

Actually, when I found out about the mission of the Tea Party and why they were initially formed - because of the bogus presentation for that $750 billion dollar bailout recommended by Hank Paulson, George Bush's Secretary of the Treasury, former CEO/President of Goldman Sachs - and not a damn thing to do with race, I knew I was on the right track listening to God about becoming a Republican.

I honestly would have never known many of the falsehoods about the Democrats if it were not for the people in the Tea Party. However, somehow the press turned the Tea Party into some type of racist demons, so automatically, I had pure contempt for these people affiliated with this group and thought they were all a bunch of racists. Isn't it ironic that they were against the same thing I was against? As I mentioned earlier, the Westchester County Tea Party became some of my very closest and dearest friends. Case in point! These preconceived ideas about others are the exact exploitations that media like Breitbart live for. There may not ever have been a Holocaust if Hitler didn't use the Jewish people as the scapegoat and stimulus for his demagoguery. Hitler needed a scapegoat for his fascist views and the Jews provided exactly what he needed. Unfortunately, these are the same tactics which still prevail and which ignited the white nationalist uprising that took place in the 2016 election. These are well thought out and calculated risk assessments based upon human behavior. Hitler knew he could sell his demagoguery to the Germans, because while they were paying reparations after WWI, the Jews were prospering, while the Germans were starving. However, this demagoguery cost Hitler the war! Hitler would have been totally justified in trying to destroy England! Hell, even America wanted to try to kill the damn English! Historically, the British Empire was and still is responsible for many of the problems in the world because of all the crimes against humanity they have committed all over the world, especially in Africa, along with the Church of England. The Church of England is a total hypocrisy! Why do you think the Pilgrims left England to come over on the Mayflower; why Martin Luther reprimanded the Church of England? Did you know the Church of England burned people at the stake for simply wanting to translate the Bible from Latin to English? Roman Catholicism, the religion that sanctioned Leopold, who murdered millions of Africans in the Republic of Congo. We never hear about that Holocaust! Now the Evangelical Right Wing is as sick as those assholes who ran the Church of

England! God, I'm afraid we have become our parents!

Hitler hated the wrong group of people! His demagoguery and rhetoric to demonize the Jews was misguided. You may ask what this has to do with the trillion dollar tax cut and/or the $750 billion dollar bailout! It's very simple. For example, I detested the Tea Party without knowing anything about them, only to find out we had many things in common. I also learned some other things that opened up my eyes to how blind I had been for the last 40 years as a Democrat! Hate blinds you to the truth, no matter what side it comes from. It's African Americans hatred towards the Republican Party that makes it virtually impossible for African Americans to see how I have come to the full knowledge and understanding of the political history of our nation. It is this blindness that the one percent rely upon to push their initiatives through, like the trillion dollar tax cut and the $750 billion dollar bailout. Actually,

African Americans have not been ignorant to the racism that permeates this society. Instead, the Republican Party has been poisoned by the carriers of this demagoguery that has now taken over the Republican Party, which is why African Americans remain in what they think is the Party that champions its causes for Civil Rights, but hasn't done anything for the last 50 years for the African American. Because in reality, that's not who they are. In actuality, the white nationalists need to go back to their original Party, the Democrats, and leave the Party that had any degree or semblance of morality. Therein lies the dichotomy. Morality! There wasn't any morality in Hitler's fascist movement! There isn't any semblance of morality in the Republican Party today. That is why white nationalists feel comfortable in this Party! And why wouldn't they, when you have an individual like Robert Mercer, who owns the right-wing fascist news medium Breitbart, controlling the entire Party?

Any nation/entity or human-being that functions without God is bankrupt, no matter how much money you may have! Please, show me where God is in fascism? This is why you need to send Breitbart and Mercer back to wherever they came from. This is the United States of America, a Christian nation, grounded in the Principles of God! Where is the killing of millions of Jews, classified or justified as Godly? Then why is the Republican Party embracing such misguided demagoguery promoted by Mercer? Simple, it's because money has become their god! If Robert Mercer, now the largest donor to the Republican Party, was spiritually minded and was a humanitarian and was truly a Christian, the Republicans would be vowing to be more humanitarian. If Mercer was for improving the public education system, the Republicans would be pushing for more improvements and money for education. If Mercer wanted healthcare for all Americans, the Republicans would be passing legislation for healthcare. However, since Robert Leroy Mercer is for extremely godless principles against humanity and is for such an ungodly belief as Hitlerian demagoguery, guess what? So are the Republicans! Therefore, if Robert Leroy Mercer is for a trillion dollar tax cut, guess what? So are the Republicans. If Robert Leroy Mercer is for a border wall, guess what, so are the Republicans! If Mercer is for detention centers at our borders so he can invest the pension funds from the American Federation of Teachers' pension that his Hedge fund runs and uses for the defense industry contractors to build and run the centers which separate children from their parents, so are the Republicans. The Republicans need Mercer's money to run their campaigns against the Democrats if they are going to have a chance in hell to win. Therefore, whatever Mercer wants, or whoever Mercer wants, even for Supreme Court Judge, like the recent appointment of Brett Kavanaugh, undoubtedly chosen by the Federalist Society, the legal arm of the Republican Party that runs on the finance of none other than Robert Leroy Mercer, then so do the Republicans, regardless of how disgusting he is. So, if you want to know what has happened to the Party of Lincoln or Lincoln Republicans, Robert Mercer is what has happened to this Party!

It would be an entirely different story if the trillion dollar tax cut was going towards causes to help the American people. It would be different if a trillion dollars was being allocated to assist Seniors who cannot afford the medicine that Big Pharma makes billions of dollars from, or small businesses, and I'm not talking about some bogus Ronald Reagan, trickle-down economics; or, if a trillion dollars were being allocated to assist those families who have mortgaged their houses over and over to ensure their children would be able to attend college! Or, even if - and the most important reason of all - even if one tenth of a trillion dollars, which would be $100 billion dollars, were to be allocated to support Homeless Veterans, disabled Veterans, mentally-ill Veterans and Veterans in general, after returning from these questionable conflicts, I could support such an undertaking. However, not one damn dime of that trillion dollar tax cut was for any of these Americans or causes for those who believe in the American way of life and its democracy and the American dream. Obviously, Mercer doesn't believe in the American Dream! However, he does believe in fascism! People like Mercer are concerned about one thing and one thing only and do not give a damn about America and/or its Democracy! If he did, how could he own Breitbart, a fascist news medium? How? It goes against everything American, unless you were in allegiance with the KKK who are those Southern Democrats who wanted to keep this nation under slavery and *Jim Crow*! This is why I previously stated, that if African Americans really came to the full revelation and understanding about the role of the Democrats in American Society and how Lyndon Johnson voted against every piece of Civil Rights legislation that ever crossed his desk while he was Senator of Texas, you would never vote for a damn Democrat! If you knew that Andrew Johnson, Lincoln's Vice President, a Democrat, repealed and replaced every piece of legislation drafted by Abraham Lincoln and the Emancipation Proclamation, you would never vote for a damn Democrat! If you knew that President Woodrow Wilson, a Democrat, refused to sign anti- lynching legislation and appointed all Southern Democrats to his Cabinet and in his Administration, you would never vote for a damn Democrat. And since you already know about Lyndon Baines Johnson, racist Texas Senator, why the hell do you think Kennedy would choose such a racist to be his Vice President? Just so you also know, Kennedy did not like Martin Luther King Jr., nor did LBJ! Now tell me, what African American in his right mind would vote for a Democrat after knowing this information? Problem is, is that after Kennedy allegedly got King out of jail, Blacks overwhelmingly joined the Democratic Party and supported Kennedy in the upcoming presidential election against Richard Nixon, who is said to have done more for affirmative action than Kennedy or Johnson, even if he was impeached!

However, since Blacks were duped into becoming Democrats, the Party of Southern racists, all the racist, fascist whites began a mass Exodus into the Republican Party. This is what I refer to as the initial symptoms of first stage cancer in the Republican Party. This is how the Republican Party, the Party of Lincoln, the Party of morality, became poisoned! Now people like Robert Mercer control the Party, its policies and laws the Party brings up for legislation. The legislation is never to support the American people, only the one percent! Sure, Mercer wants to keep white nationalism alive: however, if you are an American Taxpayer, you are not exempt from having to pay for Mercer's **Trillion Dollar Tax Cut!**

It's just like those people in England who are loyal to the Queen! They line up in the streets just to see the Queen and the royal family, as if the royal family really gives a damn about the peasants and the unemployed who are barely surviving. It's insane, but they love the Queen. Personally, I would love the Queen, only if the royal family liquidated all their ill-gotten wealth from the slavery they instituted all across the world. However, ain't no way on God's earth the royal family will ever do something as crazy as that! Yet these people worship the Queen. They stand outside to get a look at the next prince born, as they stand outside on the balconies of their castles that they own all throughout England, that the people of England pay for. You know what, Hitler should have blown England off of the face of the earth! OMG! Did I just say that? Lol! Seriously, follow closely! Case in Point! As a Black man, why wouldn't I want England destroyed? The reality is, damn near every nation in the whole world who have been oppressed, murdered, brutalized under the name of the Queen, should want England blown off the face of the earth! Hatred towards England is more than justifiable! Killing of the Jews was not! Therefore, as I previously stated, Hitler's fascism was misguided and cost him the war! However, you have those who still believe in German superiority and supremacy and want to resurrect a flawed ideology. After facing defeat in WWII, America emerged as the supreme power. America, through its ideology of democracy has become the greatest nation to ever grace the earth and that is because of its belief in God. Sure, there are problems, but even with its problems, people flee these communist, extreme religious countries, all over the world to come to America! America does not need a Mercer, with his flawed misguided ideology! He is an enemy of the State! He is an enemy to our democracy! He is successful because of our commitment to America's Democracy! Yet everything he does and supports, is against America's Democracy! And he presently controls all of the politicians in the Republican Party and every facet of our government, especially Donald Trump in the White House and Mitch McConnell in the Senate. Paul Ryan would be on that list, but he is leaving, now that the Democrats control the House. I wonder if Mercer controls any of the Democrats.

Regardless of how flawed Mercer and his right-wing doctrine he is promoting through Breitbart may be, it is successful because Mercer understands propaganda, just like Hitler did. That is why Mercer also owns Cambridge Analytica, the data mining company responsible for the data compilation targeting the right wing fascists for the 2016 election, plus his people sit on the board of Mark Zuckerberg's Facebook, both of whom came on center stage for interference with the 2016 election and Russian collusion. We all think that Russians were the brains in formulating the algorithms and targeting Americans to vote for Trump. After all, Mercer invested a huge amount of money to undertake and renovate Trump's campaign, starting with the removal of Mannefort and replacing him with none other than Steve Bannon, who runs Breitbart for Mercer and is his Vice President for Cambridge

Analytica. Remember, none of this is coincidental, but highly organized and orchestrated by someone of an extremely high intellect, although, for all intents and purposes, severely misguided! I find it interesting that no one during these so-called investigations by the Senate and the Mueller investigations have ever mentioned Mercer's name. It's a known fact he owns Breitbart! It's a known fact that he owns Cambridge Analytica. However, neither Mercer or Steve Bannon have been investigated for their role in the manipulation of the 2016 election. That's why Russia continues to say they did nothing in the 2016 election, because, in actuality, it was really Robert Leroy Mercer!

CHAPTER 5

WHY HILLARY LOST IN 2016
CAMBRIDGE ANALYTICA/FACEBOOK
RUSSIAN COLLUSION/JAMES COMEY
BENGHAZI…..

After all was said and done, the 2016 election was probably the biggest fiasco in the history of United States politics, next to the debacle that took place in 2000 with Jeb Bush stealing the election for his brother George! The reality television show, featuring none other than the clown of the three-ring circus, Donald Trump emerged as the victor of the Republican Primary. What a void in leadership in the Republican Party! It was actually insane. No matter which Republican candidate emerged, it looked like the next President of the United States of America was going to be Hillary Rodham Clinton. It was looking like a landslide victory for Hillary until an internal challenge came from the inside of the Democratic Party, by none other than Bernie Sanders, going around preaching Socialism. However insane that was, it took root and Bernie amassed a tremendous following, one that was unanticipated by the Democratic Party who had already decided that Hillary was a shoe-in for the nomination. Not so fast Hillary! Hillary just knew she was finally going to have her heart's desire, especially after being thwarted by Barack Obama in 2008. Eight years she waited for this opportunity. However, politics is a strange business.

The Republicans being aware that Hillary would probably emerge as their nemesis, began their campaign to expose Hillary's weaknesses. One serious weakness was how she handled Benghazi! How can someone expect to be Commander in Chief of the Armed Forces of the most powerful nation on earth and handle what happened at Benghazi so terribly incompetently? First test, Senate Hearing Committee which has a Republican Majority, was about to grill Hillary like red meat on a barbeque. Make no mistake about it, when those Good- Ole Boys smell blood in the water, you can best believe, you are about to be eaten alive!

Hillary's response of, 'it happened, get over it' sounded tough but I, myself being trained at some of the highest levels in terrorism took serious exception to her remark, as did many of the families who lost loved ones because of the incompetent way in which Benghazi was handled! I had no sympathy whatsoever concerning what fate awaited Hillary after such an arrogant response, with such depraved indifference. That is also the point in time when I realized that being president was important, but not as important as Commander in Chief.

Actually, that's when I really began to believe it would be possible for me to be the next POTUS in 2016 because, first of all, I had more experience and training for the War on Terror than any of the candidates, Democrat or Republican, combined with the 25 years spent in Corporate America - even if I ended up suing Texaco, Inc. for racial discrimination - along with my experience as Director of Emergency Services and Master's Degree in Public Administration, my resume was looking pretty good, especially being a Black Republican. I knew I could beat Hillary if I would be able to get Blacks to vote for me in this election. I knew I could do that, especially since the reason why I left the Democratic Party was because they hadn't done anything for the African American people for over the last 50 years, even with an African American President. With that as the case scenario, I knew the 2016 election would be no contest. Without the Black vote, Democrats cannot and will not win any national election, especially the presidency. With Donald flirting with the idea of being POTUS, I knew without a shadow of a doubt I was a far better candidate, any day of the week, and any month of the year than Donald could ever be! If only I could get my hand on one Super-PAC! When I finally reached the threshold to become eligible, there were so many people running on the Republican ticket, I was shocked, but I went ahead in spite of the crowded field of millionaires and high profile names. I had a connection that was far better than any of those other candidates seeking the presidency. Now looking back, can you imagine if Ben Carson became President, or Rudi Giuliani? Jesus Christ! Lord, help us all! The 2016 Primary was a disgrace to the Republican Party: not because I didn't win, although with God as my inside connection, integrity and decency would have prevailed over money and special interest.

Nevertheless, we ended up with Donald as the front runner, and all he consistently showed was his level of ignorance and lack of intelligence. It is said, 'it is better to be thought of as a fool than, to open up your mouth and remove all doubt!' Hillary had to be licking her chops when, clearly a fool emerged as the front runner for the Republican Party. The Republicans were surely bound to lose this election to Hillary. The Republicans, with their lack of diversity and inclusiveness were doomed. I knew I could save the Party with the ability to secure the African American vote, even though African Americans think the Republican Party are a bunch of racists. This was the opportunity to change America and change the Party. Historically, it has always been Blacks and Whites working together for the betterment of this country, ever since the Emancipation Proclamation. Well, we have to remember what that Democrat, Andrew Johnson did to destroy everything the Emancipation Proclamation represented! Maybe we could have gone 'Back to the Future' so the Republican Party could live out its original purpose before Andrew Johnson, who Lincoln selected to be his Vice President, repealed and replaced everything the Republican Party fought for in the Civil War.

Nevertheless, one thing I did find out while I was visiting my family in Eutawville, South Carolina during the Republican Primary was, if you didn't have the money to run television ads to fight back against the shots and heavy artillery that were being launched and fired, you didn't stand a chance. You need big money to play in this game! The Republicans were sounding like the Democrats! Part of the reason for this was because the Reality TV Host ran it just like it was a TV show and the media ate it up! No substance, no debate on the issues! Just ignorance!   Yet, it worked for Donald! Very disappointing and disconcerting for me as a Republican.   Surely the Party was in trouble. America was in even more trouble! Donald or Hillary...America was doomed! One godless candidate, and neither candidate having the proficiency to be Commander in Chief, yet alone lead this great country! What the hell is going on?

However, one man: Yup, *The Puppet Master*, probably fearing the worst, which was Hillary becoming our next Commander in Chief, came up with a strategic plan. Here are the facts! The *Puppet Master*, as I previously stated, came in, took over Donald's campaign, got rid of Manafort, brought in Steve Bannon, the Editor for Breitbart, and Kellyanne, and the rest is history my friends! The billionaire Hedge Fund owner, computer scientist extraordinaire, Ph.D, who is also the owner of Breitbart, the right wing fascist news medium, and owner of Cambridge Analytica, which Bannon is Vice President of, partnered with Mark Zuckerberg, the owner of Facebook, and began to orchestrate and conduct the 2016 election outcomes.

Seriously, you cannot believe Donald had the wherewithal to actually beat Hillary without some serious intervention! Next step was the email scandal. The Republicans do what the Republicans do best. Just like they persecuted Bill over Monica, this blatant disregard for the sexual assaults and payoffs to silence women went by the wayside. Donald even referred to a conversation caught on tape degrading women as locker room talk. With a female as his opponent, there was no way on God's earth, Donald could win. However, the *Puppet Master* is a genius. He activated his alt-right base and they came out of the cornfields to Donald's rallies. Never in the history of American politics was there such unprecedented mobilization, except maybe with the exception of Obama. The media was fascinated. Ratings had to be going off the charts. Donald has to get some credit also, because he knows how the media thirsts for entertainment. What would have sent Bill Clinton to jail, and has sent Bill Cosby directly to jail, has no bearing whatsoever on Trump! Donald is filling stadiums, but Hillary is still a viable opponent. We have to undermine her. Let's make the use of an illegal email server a major issue. All we kept hearing was the emails, over and over, again and again. Never mind that this wasn't the first time someone had used a server that was for personal purposes. No matter what the facts, this became a major issue. Again, Hillary's indifference and arrogance played right into the hands of the Republicans. Then there was Comey, the Head of the FBI conduct an investigation. As I watched the Head of the Senate Hearing Committee go in on Comey, he answered as strategically as he could without implicating himself or Hillary, probably in anticipation that she would be his next boss. After the hearing was over, there was a call to review Hillary's testimony. Comey probably realized that this could become a serious problem for him along with his testimony.

Simultaneously, there was also Benghazi, and as I said before, President is one thing, Commander in Chief is entirely another. People died because of the Obama Administration's handling of Benghazi and especially because Obama made Hillary Secretary of State, based upon what? Because of the fact that the

Democrats had to keep Hillary relevant for 2016! As one who has trained extensively in the Department of Homeland Security, with Police and Fire all over this nation, I took and still take serious exception to Hillary and Obama's Benghazi debacle. One thing having extensively trained as a Director, and Certified Instructor in Weapons of Mass Destruction and Terrorism, "At the end of the day, we all go home!" Having trained to the highest level in Incident Command Systems (ICS), I know that this War on Terror is real and I would never send troops into harm's way like George did with his invasion of Iraq and Afghanistan, sending troops in without properly armored vehicles, getting killed by roadside bombs and IEDs (Improvised Explosive Devices)! Not to mention Dick Cheney's "No Bid Contracts." This ineptness and get wealthy by sending American Troops into combat for personal gain is totally unacceptable from any Party! Now you have two pawns thinking they are qualified to hold the most prestigious office in the land. One could easily conclude these are all serious and viable reasons for Hillary to lose; but not so for a sexual predator who degrades women. With women being the highest electoral voting-block, how could Donald come close to being victorious? For Donald to win, it would take a miracle and a genius. Even the Evangelical Right, the Pharisees, intervened for Donald. This was going to take some serious intervention. Maybe even Russian Collusion? At the end of it all, Cambridge Analytica, with Facebook ads, James Comey's last minute discovery of more emails far removed from Hillary becoming an issue, and Russian Collusion cannot even begin to explain 53% of white women voting for Donald, unless the Facebook ads targeting those who may possibly support Trump were targeted to that audience, yet that is still a bit far reaching. Do I believe Russia colluded? Absolutely: however, I still do not believe that was the reason why Hillary lost. Somewhere in the background there was another candidate, funded by no other than the billionaire Koch brothers, who were very strategic in the outcome of the 2016 election and with their candidate who also had ties to the Kremlin.

Jill Stein, yeah, remember her? Who gained well over a million votes and, I guarantee, her campaign, for those votes were strategically and mainly targeted in Swing states. Just for your edification, the Koch brothers are also large donors for the Republican Party, who previously bet on the Mormon, Mitt Romney in 2012 against Obama. I also guarantee you that my good friend, Robert Leroy Mercer, who I actually admire for his intellectual superiority, ran the algorithms, to determine which states needed to be won to win the Electoral College. I assure you, he knew Trump didn't have a chance in hell of winning, unless he won the Electoral College. I am also sure that the *Puppet Master* orchestrated and coordinated the whole band of players to reach the desired outcome. In essence, he outsmarted the Democrats with his strategy, and at the same time has remained anonymous! While Cambridge Analytica was being investigated, you never once heard the name Robert Leroy Mercer. You did hear Mark Zuckerberg. Zuckerberg has been summoned back to Parliament for lying to the British Parliament about the impact of Facebook's ads in the Brexit debacle that has the Prime Minister ready to be thrown out of office with a vote of No Confidence, while the owner of Cambridge Analytica sits back and lets the music play like a well-trained orchestra. Yup, one man and his billions, controlling the United States of America, from the White House to the Senate, to the Supreme Court! If only he believed in the democracy of the country he came to as an immigrant himself, or at least his parents came to. Sad, really sad! Mercer could do such great things with his wealth for America and its democracy! Instead he opts for a trillion dollar tax cut for the one percent! He could be such a philanthropist! Hey, but we continue to love the Queen! We continue to vote for the Elite, who could care less about the average American.

Why do we continue to vote for these politicians who are controlled by the one percent! I do realize how important money is for campaigns and if you are running for office you are going to need a fortune to run an effective campaign and so we are compelled to go to the likes of Mercers and the Koch brothers. It's like having to go to the Godfather. You owe, plain and simple. You have to pay if you take the money. What other choice does one have? I understand that Bloomberg, the former billionaire mayor for the City of New York, who forced the City Council to change the rules pertaining to term limits so he could run for a third term, is now donating several million dollars to the Democrats. Also instituted Stop and Frisk and I hear he is thinking about running for President in 2020. If Blacks vote for him after what Stop and Frisk did to African Americans as a people.... So between Russian Collusion and Billionaires controlling our politics and the direction of our democracy, what can a civil minded public servant do? I guess nothing, but take the money! However, as long as we have people running algorithms like Cambridge Analytica and Facebook targeting people with ads, the propaganda will go on and on and on. It really has boiled down to who has the best Public Relations and Marketing team to discern the analytics, and that takes money, lots of money! Oh yes, there is always Breitbart! Whatever it is, they continue to make us believe that they are not under the influence of the one percent and are for the American people and its democracy. Beware of the propaganda. George used it to get us into a war in Iraq that has continued for over 15 years already. Propaganda. He used 9/11 to convince America to invade Iraq and in actuality, it was the Saudis; but the Bush family was in bed with the Saudis and they were the only ones allowed to fly out of the country on 9/11 when all flights were grounded. Yet, we sped into Iraq for George's own personal vendetta over Saddam and his father. Now we have ISIS and all kinds of Terrorist groups in the Middle East!

You do realize that Haliburton and these defense contractors made a fortune from that war at the expense of American lives, and now when our soldiers come home, we don't have any jobs for them. We do not have a place for them to live. We do not get them the medical assistance they need. The VA is understaffed and we do not deal with their PTSD from the horrors of war they have experienced! Yet, we can sanction a trillion dollar tax cut for these damn elitists. America, we are better than that. Let's get serious and let's take back our country from these elitists. Let's stop buying into the propaganda and the rhetoric, and let's take back our democracy - the democracy that the Republican Party was forging toward with the creation of the Emancipation Proclamation. It's what separates America from every other nation in the history of the world.

Let's make 'God Bless The United States of America', more than just a slogan!

CHAPTER 6

PROPAGANDA

Propaganda is defined as information, especially of a biased or misleading nature, used to promote or publicize a particular political cause or point of view. Sound familiar? It should. This is exactly the strategy that the rich and powerful have been using consistently throughout history and increasingly since WWI. Actually, WWI was the first war where propaganda was used at an increasingly significant rate to allegedly inform the public about the war, but more so to influence and shape their thinking about the role of America in the war. The powers that be continue to use propaganda for their agendas. Today, propaganda is used for everything. You name it, and propaganda is right there. The pharmaceutical companies have Americans taking all kinds of medications for all kinds of illnesses. Their commercials portray these wonderful scenes of serenity and peacefulness, and then they tell us in a soft, quiet, soothing voice about all the side-effects that will ultimately kill you from taking this medication, while they continue to make billions pushing their experimental drugs on the American people and the world. Monsanto and Dow Chemical sell us cancer causing Genetic Modified Organisms (GMO) as food, then sell us the drugs for the cancer they caused in the food chain from the GMO which, by the way, are not required to be identified on the labels of food packaging! They lobbied hard against the FDA for labeling and paid whoever was in charge in Congress or in the Senate to make sure identifying GMOs is not required on food labels. My question to these producers of this unnatural food is, if it is safe, then why not identify it on the packaging? I think it's because if someone were to track GMOs they would probably be able to distinguish a direct correlation to cancer and the GMO, which could lead to huge lawsuits! The point of bringing this to the forefront is because no matter how smart you may believe you are, you are basically defenseless against the deep psychological studies and applications designed to shape the human cognitive reaction. Companies spend millions of dollars to shape the way we think. They use all different kinds of media and advertisements through television and radio, Hollywood and music, to shape and determine how we may or may not respond.

The same principles apply in politics, although maybe even deeper and darker. Just like George used 9/11 to manipulate the United States into one of the most costly wars in the history of the world. Everyone knew it was an attempt to control the oil. People forget the Bush family are in the oil industry. Hence, the relationship with the Saudis.

Politically, Blacks loved Bill Clinton; however, do they realize it was Clinton who came up with the "Three Strikes Law?" And Black people wonder why so many of us are in prison! What about Clinton's welfare reform? Such bullshit! Especially in an economy where there weren't any jobs! Get off of welfare and go work where? I think Blacks have been damaged the most by following and believing in the propaganda of the Democrats more than any other group of people. This is why I am trying so hard to help Black people to understand that their future is within the Republican Party, regardless of the fact that presently, this puppet who is in the White House.

Imagine, thirty percent of Latinos still voted for Trump, regardless of the extremely derogatory statements he made about them as a people. In actuality, I find that to be quite asinine. I remain still somewhat perplexed how 53% of white women voted for Trump, except for the fact that voting for Hillary was even worse. Then why not vote for Jill Stein?

Somewhere, someone had determined that if 53% of white women voted for Jill Stein that would still, theoretically speaking of course, leave us with Hillary. Like I said earlier, the *Puppet Master* understood the implications and ramifications of the entire outcome of the 2016 election, because, I am absolutely sure, the "Computer Scientist" who is and was capable of running every computerized scenario to figure out how Donald could win the election, realized he was going to need some assistance, and through collusion with Russia, Cambridge Analytica's analytics, the billionaire Koch brothers who financed Jill Stein, calculated what states would need to be won electorally, and those were the states where Jill Stein was heavily promoted, supported and funded, to target potential Hillary votes.

In my opinion, Hillary and Donald were the two worst candidates for President ever in the history of the United States. It was a well-orchestrated accomplishment, however, at the detriment of the American people and its democracy. Truly, damned either way! Although, you have to admit, Robert Mercer is one smart SOB!

Regardless, neither Party had an economic plan that was going to be for the betterment and improvement of life for the American People. For all those people chanting "Lock Her Up!" And "Build A Wall," "Lock Him Up" could very well apply to Trump and also to many people who have close ties to his administration. Now, Flynn who led the chant, "Lock Her Up," is headed to jail. Michael Cohen is also headed to jail and even Trump may be headed to jail, along with his son and son-in-law because of their collusion with Russia. The one thing we all need to be more aware of is that propaganda is a very dangerous tool in the wrong hands, especially in dictatorships associated with Communists countries.

Ironically, we do business with these dictators on the premise of "Free Trade" and turn a blind eye to the human atrocities transpiring in these countries. It's a known fact that, if you interact within an environment for an extended amount of time, you become a part of that environment. Therefore, if you do business with dictators and murderers, at some point you will become as ruthless as the ones you are in total objection to because of their disregard for humanity. Politically, if you are part of a democracy and you are deeply intertwined with an anti-democratic state, like Trump is with Putin, you will begin to exhibit similar behaviors. Isn't it ironic that there was a time when being associated with communists was political suicide? Now, because of this relationship between Trump and Putin, regardless of the enormous implications of Putin having serious and damaging information or images on Trump, Putin is attempting to control Donald? Only thing stopping Putin in all probability, is the *Puppet Master!* Although this may be purely speculative, logistically it sounds very feasible and logical. We even sell arms to the enemies of Israel! Don't forget about the Iran Contra scandal under Ronald Reagan! Arms deals everywhere! Ultimately, too many who have now become enemies of the United States, like Osama Bin Laden!

It is totally insane to give Iran the capability to become a nuclear nation! Seriously! Oh, don't forget the bogus WMDs in Iraq! What propaganda George used to pull that one off! That's what we refer to in the field of Communications as Black Propaganda! Ironically, Black Propaganda is bad and White Propaganda is good. George W Bush straight up lied to the American people and used Colin Powell, the once highly respected General, to perpetrate his lie and his motives to get the United Nations to agree for the United States to invade Iraq. The problem is, once you go into that deep dark or Black Propaganda, there is really no return. I think this is what might have happened to Robert Leroy Mercer when he decided to own Breitbart, the "Right-wing fascist news medium!

Why has Mercer embraced that dark rhetoric of bigotry and hatred? I believe it stems all the way back to his childhood. Probably, as a little boy genius, Robert probably had very few, if any, friends. He was also probably very isolated since his parents were immigrants from Canada and migrated to New Mexico. Now, even more isolated, he probably didn't have any girlfriends and was probably also bullied. Sort of like the Television show Young Sheldon or The Big Bang Theory. He definitely didn't have any supermodels chasing after him because he was super smart. We know that for all intents and purposes they look for rich idiots like Donald! I can see Mercer sitting there crying and saying to himself, 'One day, you just wait and see, I am going to rule the world and all these bastards will pay!' They all will bow down to me!' Heil Hitler!!!

If you ask any kid why he joined a gang, he will say because they treat him like family. This is just my unprofessional theoretical psychological synopsis of what happens to a little boy who is so smart that he is actually isolated from all social interaction. For me, at least I was able to play sports. Girls always liked guys who played sports, especially basketball, which actually, I was horrible at for a very long time. However, since girls liked basketball players, I was determined to excel in the sport and if it wasn't for a girl who I fell so deeply in love with as a teenager, I probably would have had a scholarship to play college basketball and would probably be married to one of those supermodels or actresses or singers, if I had made it to the NBA!

Let's be honest, we all know a lot of those guys in the NBA are not that attractive, but when you have NBA money you can end up with a beautiful wife! Personally, I would always have to ask the question, would she be with me if I didn't play ball and make all this money? Kind of goes back to the beginning of this story about Kanye and Kim, Donald and Melania! For the latter, we really know the answer now more than ever.

Robert Mercer is now one of the most powerful men in the whole world because he controls the most powerful country in the whole world. Actually, when you think about it, it is pretty awesome! However, it is extremely tainted by the path the dark, black propaganda he decided to embrace, probably as a young child that has brought him to become the owner of Breitbart. If you were to take Breitbart out of the equation, there is no telling what incredible contributions Mercer could have made to humanity. The sad part is that, now he is a Republican. The other sad part is that the dark propaganda is now the poison which has permeated the Party of Lincoln. I equate dark propaganda with Satan. It's that voice that whispers in your ear, like the voice that caused that kid to go shoot up the church in Charleston, South Carolina. It's what must be that deep darkness inside of every man that can cause someone to get in his car at Charlottesville and mow people down and unfortunately ended up killing a young woman! It's that darkness that causes men like Hitler to kill millions of Jews. It's that deep dark spirit that justifies Apartheid. The darkness that drove Cain to slay his brother Abel. The same darkness which led the Pharisees to have Jesus Christ killed on the Cross! Yet my God has led me to become a part of this Party that walks in this darkness. And I will tell you this, before Donald, I knew that there was great potential for America! God gave me a divine economic vision for this country, for the people of this country!

Look, it's really very simple. All that is happening with this "Right Wing Movement" is, that a man understands he needs to work in order to feed his family. If you outsource four million American jobs to other countries, guess what happens? There are more people than jobs and if you have millions of people entering this country, legally or illegally, there are far more people than jobs, and now you have a major problem. Fertile ground for white nationalism. In reality, the only two groups of people who truly have the right to be upset with what is happening in this country are the ones who are responsible for this country's victory in WWII, and they are the Blacks and Whites! Because if it wasn't for these two groups, America would have lost the war and we would be speaking German right now! Fact!

Viet Nam was a military disaster and before Nam, MacArthur made a huge mess with American lives in Korea. WWII was the defining point for America and there were really only two groups with hundreds of thousands of men in that war. Thank God these men had the wherewithal to put aside their differences to defeat Hitler and Japan! There were others, but not to the extent and nowhere near the numbers of these two groups of men.

Compounded by the fact that, when you consider how this country treated the Black man after a million Black soldiers fought and were directly responsible for America's victory in WWII, the

Black man has the right to be more upset, even more than any white nationalist. When you look at all the inventions the Black man is responsible for in American history, we should be the ones carrying tiki torches, protesting about the injustices in America.

Can you even begin to imagine what the police response would have been if there were a mob of Blacks marching through the city of Virginia or a college campus with tiki torches? The governor probably, no not probably, would have definitely would have called out the National Guard.

I think immigrants entering into this country need to know the history of this country, more than anything else! I guess the problem would be which version of America's history should they be exposed to? Democrat or Republican? For a very long time the image of the Republican Party has been poisoned by its relationship to groups like the KKK and now white nationalism and fascism. While the Democrats paint this picture of inclusiveness. The Democratic

Party is very much isolated as far as diversity in its higher ranks; maybe even more than the Republicans! It all comes down to propaganda.

Considering there are millions of Latinos trying to enter this country by any means necessary, the Democrats are licking their chops, because it is more than likely that if they become citizens, they will vote for the Democrats. Hopefully they won't end up like the African Americans who walk around promoting the theme, "I'm a Democrat 'til I die!" I don't know where the hell that came from, but we have adopted it as part of our culture. Even I once believed that, until God led me on this amazing journey now to become a Republican, with the exception of this new schism and paradigm shift into the abyss with Donald as the President of this country. What a major catastrophe for the Party and country!

The indoctrination of propaganda by Whites or Black is dangerous and when it is religious it is ten times more dangerous! When it is religious, it limits one's

111

ability, intellectually, individually and collectively. Remember the story in the Bible of how the Chief Priest convinced the people to choose Barabbas instead of Jesus Christ? That's how dangerous propaganda is when it comes to religion. It will have you choose a sexual predator and a narcissist, or in the case of the biblical context, a murderer and a thief. That's what the Evangelical right was able to get their congregation to do. However, in all fairness, Hillary was just as bad! Yet, the Republican Party supported an ignorant fool who publicly disrespected an American War Hero like John McCain, and insult the Pope! Tell me America, where does the insanity end? Has Satan blinded you so much, that you can no longer distinguish integrity and decency?

I'm often amazed by the mental stronghold the Democrats had on my mind. I was like the elephant being held by a chain with a stake in the ground. You have no idea of how hard it was to actually leave the Democratic Party. However, when I finally broke the chain before this insane, egomaniac took over the Republican Party, I could actually say I found freedom! But now, all I know is that it is my mission to get back that freedom and bring this Party back to the Party that was the Party for equality and freedom. The Party of Lincoln Republicans! I have no idea now, what the hell this Party presently stands for. However, it definitely isn't equality and freedom! Only one thing left to do!

CHAPTER 7

PETER W SHERRILL

2020 REPUBLICAN PRESIDENTIAL HOPEFUL?

(HOW TO REALLY MAKE AMERICA GREAT AGAIN)

The floodgates have already begun to open for 2020, as every Democrat and their grandmother believe they are now capable of being POTUS, because anything and/or anybody is better than Donald! Can't say I really disagree. He has been and continues to be a disgrace to this country. It still amazes me that people still believe what he says. It's even more amazing the spin that Sarah Huckabee and FOX News put on his insanity.

However, that just goes to show you what media and propaganda do. They control what you think and how you think. It kind of reminds me of the Book of

Revelations. Even with the fire and brimstone and disasters destroying the earth, there were those who just refused to repent. The irony is that The Republicans in the Senate and formerly of the House, seem to line up just like how the Scribes and Pharisees in the Bible did. 'They marveled at the Beast!' They bore the mark of the beast! For all intents and purposes, the Republican Party is now under the control of the "Spiritually Wicked."

Actually, the Bible does speak very decisively about spiritual wickedness in high places. So, if you read your Bible, this shouldn't come as such a surprise to you. However, if you don't, then please be advised! Look at the shutdown, which hopefully will be over before this book is available on Amazon. Well, it now is over, however, now Donald is on some other insane referendum! Wonder who Donald is taking his cues from? This cannot be simply because Donald wants a 'Wall'. Not only does Donald want a 'wall,' he wants a $5.7 billion dollar 'wall!' Let's

115

take a minute to recap. Please, remember this one thing, if you do not learn anything else from this literary dissertation. Just remember, next time these thieves decide to tell you how much money they are gonna need for you to pay for their corporate cronies, because that's who are going to be the ones who are contracted for the 'wall' and any other fiascos we will end up paying for, just remember, it will take one thousand years for an American Taxpayer who earned $100,000 a year to make one billion dollars. For whatever reason, or whoever really wants this 'wall,' they are saying the American Taxpayer needs to give Donald $5.7 billion dollars to start building a 'wall!'

First of all, being a Director of Emergency Services, highly trained in Incident Command Systems (ICS), Cobra training in WMD and Energetic Materials, securing the 'Border' is not that difficult! I knew how to do it in 2016 and I know how to secure it right now and it will not cost the American Taxpayer $5 billion dollars! Oh, now the price just went up to $8.6 billion dollars. Seriously! That's how ignorant they are hoping this right wing is! They need you to stay focused on being blind and full of hate.

They continue to use propaganda in the name of National Security, these scare tactics to get the American Taxpayer to agree to these astronomical sums of money for the one percent's investment agendas. Why do you think that Donald is stuck on $5.7 billion dollars? And we all know that Mexico is not paying for the 'wall.' The secret lies in who gets the contract for this 'wall?' I will bet you any amount of money that there is a direct correlation between the defense contractors who get to build this 'wall,' and the companies that the top donors of the Republican Party have major investments in. Just like Robert Mercer and his Renaissance Hedge Fund along with Vanguard, where Mercer has just recently, extensively increased his investment in the Detention facilities on the border, where they are separating and holding children and detaining parents. This is what happens when you have an individual who thinks he is the President but is nothing more than a puppet. This is what happens when you borrow money from the devil! Eventually, you have to pay it back! One way or another.

However, do not believe for one minute that the Democrats are immune from these same tactics. Remember, in 2008, Goldman Sachs was the second largest contributor to Obama's campaign. What, you think they gave him all that money because they liked him? Hell no! They gave him all that money to make the American People believe that they needed us to give J.P. Morgan, Chase, Citicorp and all those other large banks that were too large to fail, $750 billion dollars. It is very necessary to understand what is being done to us. First of all, the average American Taxpayer only earns approximately $60,000 a year, plus you have to pay taxes on that money also. Basically, it would take well over a thousand years to earn just one billion dollars. That's over fifty generations. Imagine how many generations it would take for the next generations to pay back $750 billion dollars for these financial demons on "Wall Street?" Plus, we had to pay these - excuse me for one second - we had to pay these bastards bonuses for driving us into bankruptcy. After which, these bank executives wouldn't even give the average American Taxpayer a loan and still repossessed many American Families' homes! Not to mention GM and the auto industry along with the airlines. Hell, today GM is laying off 15,000 workers, after we have given Corporate America another trillion dollars and a tax cut for life! Now you can't even book an airline ticket and select a seat without paying an extra fee, or sit next to a family member, even a child during a flight, without paying an extra fee, and God forbid you have a suitcase! This is what we have paid for America, whether you are Black or White, and our politicians, both Democrats and Republicans, have sold their souls to be able to stay in power, only for the benefit of the one percent who represent America!

You know, nothing changes until you get sick and tired of getting the short end of the stick and that's putting it mildly! Actually, unless we unite, this Democrat vs. Republican battle will rage on and the American Taxpayer will always end up bearing the brunt of these economic hardships. I believe the reason why we ended up with Donald is because this was Satan's last attempt to destroy the Party that can do what is right for the Nation! Robert Mercer is the *Puppet Master,* and he is doing Satan's bidding. He sold his soul long ago when he decided to become owner of Breitbart. Breitbart is anti-American, anti-Democracy, anti the pinnacles of the American Constitution. Yet you have these conservatives who are in the Federalist Society talking about they want to go back to the original contextual meaning of the Constitution written by the Forefathers. The Conservatives are always talking about Laissez Faire

Economics and a Laissez Faire Government, however, when the Great Depression of 1929 hit, what happened to Laissez Faire Government and Economics then? That economic theory which was bullshit then and is bullshit now, went straight to hell. Same thing in 2008! Conservatives talking about government spending and the sequestering of all government agencies to reduce spending by 10 percent! Now Republicans are running the government and have not only given Corporate America and the one percent a trillion dollar tax cut for life, they have approved the highest tax spending bill in the history of this nation, and guess who gets to pay for all of this economic bullshit? We do! As an Economics major, I believe this is an outrage! When does it end...or does it?

"Houston we have a problem!" As long as we have billionaires funding both sides of the "Aisle" not a damn thing is going to change! Here is the irony. If you really believe that the elite are going to do anything to jeopardize their status, you are seriously mistaken. The Elite will always look out for the Elite. This is a game to them; almost like Eddie Murphy and Dan Akroyd in the movie Trading Places. Only difference is, in real life the one percent control the politicians on both sides of the "Aisle!" The question now becomes, is there any hope for the future of our democracy, or will we become like our 'parent', England, a shell of the government we used to be, bogged down in rhetoric and battles that benefit no one in the country! While we ponder the future of our democracy, remember, just as I said in 2016 when I was seeking the presidency, not realizing that the billionaires were actually controlling who could and would not be able to afford to play, "The Terrorists are watching!" One thing I knew for sure was that terrorism was and is real! Let me reiterate, as a former Director in this field and in Emergency Services for my local municipality I have had the honor and the privilege to train with some of the best of the best in the field of Homeland Security, in Terrorism and Weapons of Mass Destruction.

I know that undocumented immigrants are a real problem, especially on our Southern Border and having been extensively trained in Homeland Security, I understand that Border Security is no joke! I share in the concerns this poses for our Nation! Also, you have to understand that entering this country illegally allows for drug trafficking and prostitution, child trafficking, and child pornography and all other types of illicit activities one may be forced to become subjected to because of being here illegally, not being able to qualify legally for employment. This is the reality of life in America.

According to the last count there were over 11 million undocumented illegal immigrants in this country, so building a 'wall' is akin to 'closing the barn door after the horse has bolted!' We needed a 'wall' a very, very, long time ago. Now Donald is trying to force America to build his 'wall' because he got his alt-right supporters to chant their ABC's, 1,2,3. "Build A Wall, Build A Wall." Seriously, so now the American Taxpayer is supposed to build a $5.7 billion dollar wall because of that? "Get the hell outta here with that asinine ignorance!" How damn ignorant do you think the American people are?

Nevertheless, the government was shut down over this alleged security threat. Truth is, if you really wanted to control the security at the border, there is a much more efficient and effective way to do it. If I don't know anything else, I do know security. I was trained by the best in the business, at Anniston Alabama, Fort McClellan, COBRA Training and at New Mexico Tech, Energetic Materials Research Training Center for Counter-Terrorism First Responder Training. I would tell you what I would do, but if I did, then the Democrats might steal it because they do not know how to govern, so they steal! Actually, all politicians steal, even Republicans. Actually, Donald would have to also, because he doesn't have a clue as to what the hell he is doing in the first place. This is why things are presently in disarray in Washington, because no matter how much money you may have, there are some elements in and of government you just cannot control. You need someone who has a comprehensive understanding of how things work. Which is why I studied hard when I was in government and trained harder! It's one thing to know the material you are being taught, it's quite another thing when you have to practice what you have learned. This was one area I strongly emphasized when training with Police and Fire. You respond how you train, and even though they would sometimes think I was a pain in the ass, I always lived by the code that, at the end of the day we all go home. In (ICS), if done properly, things work out every time. I believe that if ICS was being followed, these police shootings of young black men would not occur! If you look at every shooting in America, or every incident where a Firefighter was injured or killed, I guarantee you that they had never been to Anniston for COBRA Training or to New Mexico Tech for the Counter-Terrorism Training at the Energetic Materials Research Training Center.

First of all, you have to be at a certain level of training in Incident Command Systems. The very basic level at the Police Academy is level 100 and most Police and Firefighters are not inspired to go beyond that training, and because of that, they really do not understand how to respond to incidents, other than emotionally, and charged with adrenaline. I've published stories on 9/11 and Firefighters, about being under a cloud of smoke and being on the "Pile" right after the Towers came down, without basic level C, Personal Protective Equipment on. I've trained with Chiefs of Departments and one day had to challenge my own Deputy Chief on why he would send men in, given the conditions that were given in the training scenario we were evaluating. As we discussed the pros and cons of why and why not, that's when I said, "At the end of the day, we all go home!" I felt especially validated when all the officers from the NYPD said, "We want him with us." However, when the scenario continued and the explosion occurred, I said to my Deputy, "Now you have to go explain to those families why you sent them in under those hazardous conditions and you knew their PPE would break down in a matter of two minutes. There was no justification, except if you were trying to be a hero!" "Study hard, train harder!" Incident Command Systems basically prepares every Responder how to be safe and effective at all times. It also will provide insight on how to handle all types of events, Sporting or Concerts or even the 'wall.' Actually, a 'wall' makes you lazy. It gives you a false sense of security. These are things I know, because I have trained in the field and have studied hard and am a Certified Trainer in Response and Terrorism. As far as the border, and Trump's 'wall,' I can guarantee that if the American people would allow me the honor of being Commander in Chief, there would no longer be a border problem in America.

The one thing we must be cognizant of, is the fact that undocumented entry into this country is illegal, and as Commander in Chief, if you come into this country illegally, there will be serious consequences. Illegal immigrants would wish a 'wall' was their only obstacle. The border would be on serious lock-down! This 'wall' is a ploy to give Donald and his "Boys" a valid excuse to have the American Taxpayers finance another one of their ventures in capital! $5.7 billion dollars worth of capital! Again, now it's $8.6 billion dollars. How about finding $5.7 billion dollars to help our Veterans and the families who have lost loved ones in this freakin bogus war George W. got us into in the first place and spent trillions of the American Taxpayers' dollars going after the wrong guy because the Saudi family, who are believed to have committed this act of terror against us have deep ties to the Bush family! And they wanted

America to vote for Jeb, after all the economic destruction George put this country through.

Initially, Jeb was the leading candidate for the Republican Party. Honestly, Hillary would have probably eaten Jeb alive! At least my strategy to lead an exodus of the African American people out of the Democratic Party could have been the beginning of how to really make America great again, like after WWII. But Jeb? Have you seen Ted lately? And Rudy has lost his cotton-pickin' mind; not to mention Ben Carson! All of those were candidates in 2016 and would have lost to Hillary. However, I know without a doubt, Blacks would have left the Democrats to vote for me if I had won the Republican Primary. Just one Super PAC! That's all, just one! Hell, just one television interview! I figured with my educational background in Economics and Master's in Public Administration, combined with my 25 years of experience in Corporate America and extensive training in Homeland Security, minus the propaganda, my economic vision for America was great then and is still great now, and definitely better than any of those candidates, Democrat or Republican, could have ever implemented! A trillion dollar tax cut for corporations doesn't benefit the American Taxpayer. Tariffs, don't benefit the American Taxpayer either. It would cost the American Taxpayer more money to survive everyday. I just keep forgetting that in politics, it doesn't have a damn thing to do with qualifications. It's all propaganda!

Mussolini, a journalist, the father of the fascist movement, used propaganda to control the people of Italy and led them to war against Ethiopia when he ran out of options and people were running out of food, to recapture that sense of nationalism amongst Italians. It was amazing to watch how he rose to power through the use of propaganda and the media as a journalist and was respected and admired by none other than Adolph Hitler! After Mussolini's invasion of Ethiopia by Italy once again, and the use of chemical weapons supposedly banned by the Geneva Convention, Mussolini killed hundreds of thousands of Ethiopians with these banned chemicals while the Allied Forces stood idly by! It really makes me wonder if the Americans who are following and have partnered with these groups, really understand the origins, premise and the ideology fascism was founded upon? It makes me seriously question how someone as brilliant as Mercer is a sponsor of such hatred and has basically taken control of our democracy in America, using a clown who is a disgrace to America and the International Community. Even the Koch brothers are not that diabolical. At least when they financed Romney, even though there were tremendous concerns about his religious affiliation with Mormonism, the people decided the vote. Robert Leroy Mercer has taken this quest for power to a whole new low in relationship to democracy! Democracy and fascism do not mix. They are not related and these conservatives are seriously misguided, trying to disguise fascism as democracy.

Now, when it comes to religious freedom, well that's another story. I'm not sure that the Founding Fathers, when crafting the Constitution, meant any religion that you believe in qualifies under the Constitution of the United States categorically as acceptable in this country. All I'm saying is that if you understand Judaism and its principles, and how God felt about the worshipping of false gods and idols, you might be very reluctant to have all these different religious practices invading your sanctuary! Case in point! Take Mormonism, they believe that God is going to return to Missouri. I'm not saying that God can't if he so chooses, but where in the hell did that indoctrination come from? Mormonism is more noted for its racist practices and views than its morality! From a spiritual perspective, I'm not sure if God really recognizes Mormonism. However, Mitt Romney donates somewhere in the region of 4 million dollars to the Mormon Church of Jesus Christ of Latter Day Saints and is a high ranking official in their ceremonial practices. Many people wonder what those ceremonial practices are, because they are very secretive about what they do, especially with regards to the dead! Sounds more demonic than spiritual!

Personally, I have taken a look at the Book of Mormons and ain't nothing biblical about that book! At least with fascism, we know there ain't nothing godly in it! We need to seriously sit down and decide what we want our country to look like in the future. Are we a Christian nation or are we a nation that is godless, and couldn't care less what you believe, but because we are allegedly a democracy, you can come here and practice anything you want!

Presently, America as well as China are what we would consider wealthy, but they are not anywhere near prosperous! There is a big difference between being wealthy and being prosperous! My goal is to see America prosperous as a nation! You cannot be prosperous as a nation if the nation is living with, or is surrounded by ungodliness. What Robert Mercer has done to the Republican Party is surrounded it with ungodliness. The Republican Party, the Party of Lincoln was not an ungodly Party. It was a Party of morality and decency. Now we have gone from the Party of the Emancipation Proclamation, to the Party of Charlottesville, tiki torches and white nationalism! America, we are better than that! I know we are! Right now, all Donald is doing is making it easier for the Democrats to have total control of the government, and personally, I know that whatever the Democrats do, it is not going to benefit the African American people or our country. Therefore, I cannot sit idly by like the Allied Forces did with Mussolini, while America's Democracy is threatened and my people continue to be the victims of the Democrats' indoctrination. Yet, if the Republican Party continues down this path of white nationalism and its cancerous ideology, not only will the Democrats take control, but this nation and its economy, will be doomed!

This is why I will be announcing my candidacy for President of the United States for the upcoming election in 2020 and the first thing I am going to do as President of the United States is pay back the American people all the money that has been stolen from them for the last 20 years, starting with the Iraqi War manufactured by George W. Bush!

Until then, America: God Bless you and God Bless The United States of America!

CPSIA information can be obtained
at www.ICGtesting.com
Printed in the USA
BVHW041532090819
555498BV00002B/269/P